Scrum: A Story of Transformation

FOR ALL LEADERS WHO INSPIRE US WITH THEIR COURAGE TO MOTIVATE CHANGE...

Thanks

Mehmet Yitmen
Thanks to Ken Schwaber, Dave West, James Coplien, Gunther Verheyen, Tolga Kombak, Jörn Kolodzey, and all the friends, teams, and organizations that inspired me!

Thanks to Ömer Güneş, Seb haigh, and Natasha Haigh for their great efforts in translating the book into English!

I would also like to offer my gratitude and respect to Ken Schwaber and Jeff Sutherland, for gifting us with Scrum.

Ömer Güneş, Seb Haigh, & Natasha Haigh
We'd like to thank Mehmet for contributing his work to this project, even when the promise looked unlikely to be realized.

Forward

Implementing Scrum is not easy. It is not easy for the Scrum Team. It is not easy for the organization that the Scrum Team works within, and it is not easy for the stakeholders working with the Scrum Team. So why do we do it? Because we have to. Delivering value in the face of uncertainty and building a great place to work is the ultimate goal of Scrum. However, like giving up smoking or sticking to a weight loss program, it is not easy.

In this book, Mehmet narrates the story of a Scrum transformation through the eyes of Hakan, a Scrum Master and change agent. By telling the story from Hakan's point of view, he makes the challenges of transformation feel both real and personal. The journey that Hakan takes is a journey that we all face when introducing agility. First, there is the realization that the challenges he sees every day can be removed. Then sharing these ideas with others and getting support. The pilot project comes next, followed by learning and improvement. Finally the destination of enterprise adoption. Only when you get to that destination do you realize that actually the journey can continue and you are never done. Throughout the narrative, Mehmet introduces practical guidance and patterns that readers can employ in their specific circumstances.

The story of Hakan may not be everyone's story, but I am sure there are moments in the narrative where the reader will think, "Ha, that happened to me, and I wish I had done X". Such moments make this book not only more accessible, but also an opportunity for reflection.

Adopting Scrum is not easy, but it can be successful and can go from one team to many. It can change organizations allowing them to be responsive and humane. It can deliver innovation and business success, but it can only do this if people implement the ideas. Scrum requires people, and this is a story about people. Too often we forget that when talking frameworks, patterns, and practices. People are what make Scrum a success or failure and this book provides a great story about the people involved.

Thank you, Mehmet, for sharing this story. and I hope others enjoy it. Scrum On!

Dave West, CEO Scrum.org

Forward

Imagine working for a company that has many and serious problems in delivering software products and projects. Do you recognize the symptoms: always late, always over budget, and never delivering what people were hoping for? Imagine that this has been going on for a very long time, and—even worse—still goes on. It is a vicious circle that seems impossible to break. Unfortunately, this is not hard to imagine for many people and organizations.

Now imagine introducing Scrum as a different way of working. Imagine the courage it takes, as well as the excitement that it can lead to. Can you do that, imagine Scrum working in your organization? The changes that would bring about? The friction that might cause?

Mehmet Yitmen is an experienced consultant and Scrum practitioner, and he has been there. Mehmet has combined and made available his insights and experience for you as a fiction story; a transformation tale. Although the company is fictitious, the story is highly recognizable.

Mehmet describes what you might subsequently go through and how that feels during the process of implementing Scrum: the steps, discoveries, difficulties, the pleasures and the pains. He shines a light on what you might encounter on your path before and after introducing Scrum, and how to possibly respond to that; from acknowledging problems with your existing processes, to selecting a pilot project, to the different responses you might encounter, to the changes needed in culture and mindset.

Mehmet shares a tale that can help you envision a new future for you and your organization, a future where you will feel fitter and better placed to deal with unpredictability and change. Mehmet helps you the way to quickly embark on what will be a continual journey. Because, adopting Scrum is more than just a one-time effort of introducing Scrum; it is a continual exercise of thinking, rethinking, and discovery. That, in the end, is the organizational state called 'agility' that we hope to achieve by introducing Scrum.

Gunther Verheyen, Independent Scrum Caretaker

Preface

"How can we apply Scrum in our organization, and how should we start and sustain our improvement efforts?"

This is the kind of question frequently asked of me over the last decade. Whether as a speaker at conferences and seminars, a trainer, or an enterprise agile coach, it's clear that there has never been a broader or deeper interest in Scrum.

Whether the question comes from a beginning developer or an experienced business leader, there is no single, universally applicable response.

During the course of my agility consulting practice, I've worked closely with numerous companies and have coached hundreds of teams. In every company I have supported, each individual team has required a different approach to fit their specific needs.

Ultimately, Scrum is a fundamental project of change for most teams or organizations; therefore, each journey needs to be custom tailored. Scrum applies a unique mechanism and perspective, so when considering how best to apply Scrum, critical examples from my own experiences of introducing it seem not only pertinent, but crucial to illustrating good practice.

People express a great deal of curiosity about how others have implemented such change within their own teams and companies. Using examples of real experiences can help to illustrate this process. Each unique setting invites unpredictability, so it is important for each organization to first understand its own dynamics before implementing Scrum. Nevertheless, some scenarios or issues are fairly universal.

While there are dozens of books and resources in the industry about Scrum, there are few sources of guidance on how to implement it using real-life situations encountered during the implementation process. With this in mind, I set out to respond to this deficiency by sharing my own experience in order to offer guidance for those looking to apply Scrum.

I have tried to convey the process of introducing a fictitious company to Scrum, presenting the process of change in a simple, narrative form. The fictitious company I refer to struggled with constant delays in software projects and experienced difficulty in managing change. In addition, the employees were dissatisfied with the results of the projects, and the IT department lacked motivation.

In order to make the book both memorable and easy to read, I use the form of a narrative, told from the perspective of a Scrum Master, an important role in Scrum. As an initiator and leader of change, I illustrate the challenges faced by the Scrum Master, while highlighting important Scrum concepts.

My intention was not to describe Scrum in a textbook-like style but rather to illustrate the impact that the process can have on teams and organizations. This book draws attention to the process of change that Scrum enables. I hope that it inspires you to take the opportunity for dynamic growth and change within your own work and that it can serve as a go-to guide as you navigate your own unique journey.

Before reading this book, I highly recommend first studying the Scrum Guide published on www.scrumguides.org, as it offers detailed information on Scrum.

Contents

Chapter I: The Need for Change — 17
Problems and Friction — 19
No Way Out! — 24
Awakening — 28
The First Steps of Change — 31
Selection of a Pilot Project — 33
First Contact with the Business Unit — 36
Convincing the IT Department — 39
The Green Light for Scrum — 44

Chapter II: Let the Change Begin! — 47
Transformation Action List — 49
Kick-off — 53
The Team Room — 59
An Unhelpful Practice: Handing Over Ongoing Tasks — 61
Closing the Preparations — 64
Sprint 1: The First Sprint Planning — 68
First Daily Scrum — 73
The Scrum Master's Observations So Far — 76
The First Sprint Review Event — 79
The First Sprint Retrospective Event — 83
Sprint 4: The Sprint Planning Event — 89
Are Daily Scrums Really Necessary? — 93
Team Spirit — 96
Improving Communication with the Product Owner — 103
Feedback Time — 106
Evolving Transformation Action List — 109
Sprint 7: The Sprint Retrospective — 115
Sprint 9: The Sprint Review — 118
Taking Action to Spread Change — 121

Chapter III: The Wind of Change — 125
Selecting Additional Projects — 127
Six Months Later — 131

Appendices — 137
Concepts and Definitions — 138
Daily Scrum Checklist — 142
Business Satisfaction Survey — 143

Chapter I:
The Need for Change

Problems and friction

After a long day of meetings during which the participants seemed to do little more than waste time, Hakan was tired and anxious. Thankfully, the meeting madness was over, for today at least. The meetings were all the more challenging because he was simultaneously running eight projects, each of which had extended far beyond their deadlines. As the project manager, Hakan didn't see how he could possibly share so much bad news with the business units that were officially his clients.

Sure, he'd managed to postpone the reckoning for a while, putting his game face on during meetings: "Yep, the project is going well," he'd say. The more often he'd spun the truth, the more his frustration grew, but at least it bought him some time to push his project teams to address some of their issues. And unlikely though it seemed, he thought that he may be able to persuade the business unit leads to revise their expectations and shift their project plans.

With that in mind, he decided to visit Kieran in the IT department to discuss the sales reporting (SR) project, one of the many projects Hakan was responsible for managing. Yes, he thought, now's a good time to apply some pressure on Kieran and his development team. In addition to being an important figure in several other projects, Kieran was also the lead software developer on the SR project. He was involved in many areas, from setting up the project's technical structure to leading the other, less-experienced software developers. Hakan had previously worked with him on a number of projects and had come to trust in his ability to do good work. He felt that Kieran could best understand him and support him in this project.

When Hakan met Kieran, he found the entire IT team there, hard at work. Even though the work day was officially over, they seemed as fresh and focused as if it were first thing in the morning. Kieran, on the other hand, was looking past his screen, lost in thought—was it a look of boredom, or concern?

"Hi, Kieran," said Hakan. "We need to talk about the sales reporting project. I met with the business unit today, and I'm a bit fed up with telling the business folk that it's all going well, even though we're facing significant delays in the project plan. We have to finish this project on time. You know that. The top management is particularly interested in it."

Hakan sounded edgy and dissatisfied, and Kieran wasn't happy about being interrupted. He responded without taking his eyes off the screen: "I'm very busy at the moment, let's talk another time." Kieran's response was unacceptable, as Hakan was determined to have this conversation. "You don't seem to understand," he stressed, "we're in real trouble!"

But Kieran's irritation was clear: "Hakan, I'm working on an issue that I need to sort out urgently, so I can't spare any time for you today, as much as I'd like to chat. Let's talk tomorrow. Sorry about this." His terse response revealed his annoyance.

Hakan was aware that Kieran was incredibly busy and recognized that most of the responsibility for completing the project rested on him (though the development team was also giving its best efforts to the project). Still, it was not enough to ensure that the project would be completed on time. What would he say about the project to his manager, and more importantly, to the business unit? The project's timeline and milestones had been negotiated and planned with Kieran and the development team from the project's beginning. But after only four months, they had already deviated from the plan. The agreed-upon completion date was very much at risk.

Feeling stressed, Hakan turned back to Kieran, who made a show of ignoring him. Angrily, Hakan told him that he would include him in an email to both of their directors, detailing how serious the situation had become.

Hakan knew that sending this email would not be enough to resolve the issue. He had faced this sort of problem a countless number of times. For some reason, there were always delays in completing critical tasks before deadlines. Repeatedly, the team would struggle before inevitably failing to meet the agreed-upon deadlines set at the beginning of the project. This would be followed by a painful round of renegotiation, after which a new plan would be initiated; then the whole circus would begin again.

These delays made it feel like Hakan's Project Management Office (PMO) was constantly in trouble. The project managers seemed to fluctuate between pressuring the development team to fix the problems, or, failing that, trying to convince the business of the reasons for the delay and why, once again, they had to agree to a new project plan.

The repeated delays and problems across so many projects were a constant source of friction between IT and the business units. Inevitably, project managers were at the center of these hot spots. The cause of conflict was usually a variant of one side blaming the other for their delays or problems. The IT team complained that the business units did not provide clear requirement specifications and changed their minds too often. They also objected to the constant time pressure placed on them by the Project Management Office. Contrarily, the business units blamed the IT team for being too slow. According to them, constant IT delays meant that they often missed the right time to enter new markets and could not adapt quickly enough to changes in existing markets. The business team felt that the IT team didn't recognize how important it was for the company to complete their projects on time. They, too, were unhappy with the PMO, complaining that Hakan and his team were too lenient with the IT teams and too flexible in allowing changes in delivery dates. The business team wanted to be clear that the PMO was on their side, and to be assured that Hakan's team would push IT hard enough to meet the company's commitments.

Hakan couldn't help but wonder why this ongoing drama persisted. Every day there were variations of the same breakdowns in trust and communication. Ultimately, it all felt inefficient and unsustainable. The various factions seemed to spend more time arguing, negotiating, and defending than making things better for their customers and colleagues.

It was clear that they were all working to the same end: a better, stronger company that could deliver ever-greater value to its customers. Unfortunately, this common understanding and shared mission (while clear to everyone as individuals) seemed to get lost by the time the teams got down to work. It was like a cold war, with everyone taking a defensive stance that only served to make the others' work more difficult. Everyone seemed to be resigned to this cycle, accepting it as the status quo— maybe it was just the nature of the business, and perhaps the reason why project managers like Hakan were needed.

Another possibility that often crossed Hakan's mind was that it was his responsibility to keep his team on track; perhaps he was just not doing his job well enough. After a moment's self-doubt, he would reassure himself: "No, no, not at all, this is not just my problem. This is a more serious, fundamental problem that is endemic within the company. No matter how well the project managers track and intervene in projects, it isn't easy to avoid these Mexican standoffs."

Though he had no specific solution in mind, Hakan was aware of the need for more radical and permanent change within the company.

No way out!

Hakan's fruitless conversation with Kieran was almost a week ago, and his escalation email about the sales reporting project did little more than raise the temperature of the debate. Instead of inviting objectivity, involvement of the management chain had only strengthened the defensive stances of those involved, and the blame game played out with even more energy than before.

The software development team blamed the business analysts for failing to deliver on time and constantly adding new business demands to the schedule. They claimed that development delays and deviations from plans were only happening because the business analysts were not doing their job properly.

According to the business analysts, the primary source of all of these problems was the business unit. The business folk couldn't clearly communicate what they wanted and were constantly changing their minds. In addition, their new requirements couldn't possibly have as much impact on the project as the developers claimed. It wasn't realistic to pin the delays on these new requirements. Either the software development team was working inefficiently or the team was inadequate. Moreover, some additional requirements had been cancelled after negotiations with the business unit, following complaints from the software development team. The business analysts felt that it was unacceptable for the software development team to blame them while they were providing support in a chaotic environment in which the stakeholders were not clear about what they wanted.

The analysts felt that it was Hakan's responsibility to intervene and increase the software development team's capacity to accelerate the project, but Hakan knew that this wasn't possible. They were already working at significant capacity for such an important project, and at this point, adding new people to the team might not be the best solution. Even if it were a solution, it would be impossible to find such additional capacity in less than a month. Integrating new people into a project always took time, and by the time they had adapted, the project would be nearly over.

Hakan was also aware that resolution of the continuous arguing was unlikely, that complaints on all sides would not end until the project was completed, and that he, the project manager, would be held accountable. He wasn't looking for a scapegoat or trying to avoid responsibility; what mattered to him was that the project was maintained in a healthy way, with all parties working to achieve a harmonious solution. Unfortunately, as usual, this didn't happen, and blame, along with the mutual refusal to take responsibility, persisted. He knew that he should lead both parties by shouldering the responsibility. Anxiously, he tried to figure out how best to intervene.

In this case, Hakan's best step seemed to be to cover up the risk by transferring some of it to the business unit. If there was a delay in the project's completion, the effects of the delay could be minimized with advance warning, thereby avoiding a shock wave close to the deadline. In addition, if the business unit was made aware of the issues, it may prevent the possibility of having to ask for further changes in the future. Taking this into consideration, Hakan decided to arrange another project review meeting with the business unit.

In order to give the impression that things were under control, Hakan, though exhausted, entered the meeting room attempting to look cheerful and confident. Very few people from the business unit were there; apparently, Hakan thought, they must have had more important tasks to attend to.

Hakan began explaining why he wanted to meet again, only a week after their last meeting:

"I don't want to waste too much time, so let's get started. Last week, I had the chance to work more closely with the software development team, and we discussed the project in general terms. The Project Management Office is aware of how crucial this project is for you, as well as for top management and the entire company." Everyone seemed to be busy reading emails on their smartphones while pretending to listen to Hakan. He continued: "As you know, we began this project about four months ago. The first two months was an intense requirements analysis period, and for the last two months, the software development team has been developing the project. However, there have been some deviations from the project plan, with various additional requirements and changes from your side. If we continue this way, we may have to shift the project deadline a little." Suddenly, all attention was focused on him.

"Are you talking about extending the project deadline?" someone asked. "That's not an option! This is a very strategic project, and we have to launch it at the end of August, as we've discussed already!" Opposition to his suggestion was evident. Hakan nodded, visibly concerned: "I'm aware of that. That's why I wanted to warn you about the potential risk and ensure that there wouldn't be any more new requests or major changes to the project so that we can try to meet the deadline at the end of August."

Members of the business unit were clearly unhappy with the situation. "Hakan, this project must be launched on the date that we agreed! The CEO cares deeply about this project and personally tracks it! Yes, it's true that we have made some changes. Things are changing, and we have to reflect these changes within the project. Add new members to your team while you still have time, work harder, do more overtime, just do everything you can to complete this project on time! Please, don't tell us you won't meet the deadline. We asked you to have it finished by the beginning of June, but since you and the software development team thought that it was too risky and unrealistic, we extended the deadline to August. There's no way we can have any more delays!"

Hakan realized that there was no point in continuing the conversation, as the business unit would not reconsider. He decided to end the meeting so as not to increase the tension and attempted to reassure them that he would do his very best to ensure that the project would finish on schedule.

The controversy was exhausting; there was no chance of succeeding this way. The business unit was putting everyone under unnecessary pressure to complete projects earlier, and the IT office seemed unable to make a realistic time estimate and stick to it. The project management office was always between the two and always the first to be blamed at the final stage. Hakan was determined to make definitive changes.

Awakening

Almost seven months later, the sales reporting project was finally complete, having taken three months longer than expected and exceeding the budget by about 40%. Even then, the result was unsatisfactory, as the project had failed to meet all of the business unit's requirements. It was also apparent that there were issues with the quality of the software.

Software developers often spent days trying to fix unexpected problems, and meeting change requests from the business unit in anticipation of new minor features had proved challenging. Dozens of software development work tickets were still open, with a number of them having been entered into the system weeks earlier. These were all tedious delays, resulting in a never-ending project development cycle for the software team.

Hakan and the PMO no longer held responsibility for the project, since for them, it was already over. The software team was managing the change requests by itself. It was normal for such problems to persist for years, and this project was a clear example. Although Hakan was no longer involved, the inefficiencies that the project had highlighted continued to concern him.

Over the last seven months, Hakan had read up on the implementation of new methodologies and management techniques in software development projects, in the hope of finding a solution to the problems he repeatedly encountered. He was interested in the techniques applied by other companies around the world. In the course of his investigations, he had come across a concept that he remembered hearing about yet hadn't given much thought to at the time. This concept was Scrum[1].

---
[1] Scrum: A simple framework that enables people to derive value from complex challenges.

Scrum was a management framework that had intrigued Hakan from the outset. He wondered why it was defined as a framework rather than a methodology or technique. As his curiosity piqued, Hakan read books and attended seminars on Scrum, acquiring the knowledge and insight needed to convince him that it was the solution he had been looking for to provoke change and resolve the company's ongoing issues.

Yes, Scrum was the answer! But how to implement it? And where to begin? This was a completely new concept for both himself and the company, and he anticipated resistance from colleagues who would probably need to be convinced to even trial it. He decided that it would probably be best to first discuss it with his manager, and with her support, persuade the business units and IT department to give it a try. Then he could find a suitable project for which to implement Scrum, joined by a team motivated to make it work. The potential success of this project could pave the way for Scrum's implementation in other projects, allowing much-needed change to spread throughout the company.

Mei was a perfect manager who loved her work and cared about her team. Open to different ideas, supportive, and a good listener, Mei gave her team the confidence they needed to come to her with any issue. Hakan had experienced Mei's strengths as a leader when family problems were impacting his work; her sincerity and support during that time assured Hakan that he could trust her with his plans to implement Scrum. He decided to send her a brief email to introduce his idea and ask about her availability for a short discussion.

In order to prepare for his meeting with Mei, Hakan planned

a presentation that would introduce Scrum and provide empirical evidence in support of its benefits. The presentation had to explain the principles of Scrum using real-world examples and case studies, while highlighting how it could be applied to resolve the issues facing their company. With the excitement of having sent the email spurring him on, Hakan was back to work.

THE FIRST STEPS OF CHANGE

The opportunity to discuss Hakan's plans for the company had finally arrived, and Mei welcomed him warmly:

"Firstly, I'm really happy to see that you've taken the time to look for alternative solutions to the issues we keep running into, so thank you. I've come across Scrum in various posts and blogs in the last few months but haven't had much time to look at it in depth, so I'm keen to hear what you have to say."

Mei's manner was warm and encouraging, which was a huge relief to Hakan, and as he began to explain his findings, his enthusiasm and depth of knowledge had Mei captivated.

Mei had a few questions concerning issues such as who would take on the role of project manager and how the PMO would delegate and assign tasks. Hakan clarified that he would assume the role of Scrum Master[2] (if there was no objection from the team), and that he would work closely with the team to help them increase productivity in a way that was quite different to traditional project management.

The key difference between Scrum and traditional management approaches was the creation of a self-organizing team. Scrum required the team to take end-to-end ownership of projects in order to propose more creative solutions and increase team productivity. Every team member would have to take full responsibility for actively participating in the decision-making process. Hakan's role as a servant leader was to coach them to achieve self-organization and to support them in taking initiative.

---

[2] *Scrum Master: The person accountable for fostering an environment of Scrum by guiding, coaching, teaching, and facilitating one or more Scrum Teams and their environment in understanding and employing Scrum.*

Mei was impressed with the examples and supporting data, and she trusted his ability to motivate his team to adopt these new concepts. She was, however, keen to know how he would proceed with applying Scrum's principles in their company. Hakan responded confidently:

"First I have to find a candidate project. I plan to find out which business units and IT teams are open to change. If I can persuade them to implement Scrum on a project and put together a team, we're halfway there." In fact, Hakan wasn't quite sure of how to proceed with the implementation of Scrum. He couldn't predict what he would encounter. Nevertheless, he trusted the transparency at the core of Scrum, as well as the 'Inspect and Adapt' principle that he and his team would be putting into practice.

They had covered so much ground that the meeting had gone long past schedule. Mei thanked him for sharing his proposal and seemed unconcerned with the finer points of his action plan; she suggested that they reevaluate after he had met with the business units and IT people and had some feedback to share.

Selection of a pilot project

Hakan had successfully managed to pass the first stage. Now it was time to decide what kind of project to select and to whom he should suggest it. He had no time to waste; if he wanted to put his plans in motion, he knew that he should take action and contact the right people. He began to look at projects scheduled to be implemented in the near future. It was imperative that he choose the right project and team to introduce Scrum and achieve success, triggering the wind of change and extending the reach of Scrum within the company.

There were dozens of projects in the pipeline, but he quickly eliminated those that would only take a few months. These projects were too short to introduce change and achieve positive results. He also eliminated projects that were expected to take more than a year, as this would be too long to wait to prove the value of Scrum and disseminate the process according to his timescale. His focus was therefore on medium-term projects with a good scope for revealing the dynamics of Scrum—preferably those with a suitably high profile, to ensure the interest of management. Success on a project of this nature would make it easier to persuade senior management of the need for further radical change, ensuring their cooperation in his plans to expand Scrum's influence.

It was also important to find a pilot project for which he could convince both the business unit and the IT department to implement Scrum. He needed to find a project with people who could share his vision and see the potential in taking a chance on change.

One of the most obvious targets would be business units that had encountered previous problems with software projects, as dissatisfaction with the current process would make them more open to trying a different approach. Hakan also saw the need for a more visionary team within the IT unit— people like him, who were frustrated with the customary chaos and would therefore welcome new strategies.

> **Criteria for Pilot Project:**
> - ✔ Mid-sized project, expected to be delivered in 5-12 months
> - ✔ Eager business open to try a new way of working
> - ✔ Eager IT team willing to change and improve
> - ✔ Dedicated project team
> - ✔ High-profile project that has the interest of management

Hakan recognized that finding a project that perfectly matched these criteria may not be possible but waiting for the perfect project was not an option. A project that met at least some of these requirements would have to do. He felt the need to begin as soon as possible, as initiating change was essential. The current system was unsustainable and, having seen an alternative, he would not be deterred.

Among the potential projects that fulfilled some of his criteria, Hakan identified the CRM project as being a step ahead of the others; plus, his relationship with the business unit that needed this project was strong, as he had often helped them out in the past. The unit had also received complaints about software projects, since many had been subject to delays and didn't deliver the desired outcomes. Therefore, the CRM project appeared to be an excellent candidate with which to trial Scrum, and he was confident that he could persuade the business unit of the improvements that it could bring.

Kieran and his team were managing the needs of this business unit, and they would be ideally suited to working with Hakan, as they, too, were fed up with the current situation. Hakan knew Kieran very well, and he was quite confident that with his support, they would be amenable to trying a different approach, especially one that promised to reduce the consistent pressure and stress that they were under.

In addition, this was an important project for senior management. It was being overseen by the deputy general managers, who were keen to push the project forward as soon as possible.

Delighted that he had found an excellent pilot project for which to apply Scrum, and confident that Mei and the IT department could easily be persuaded, Hakan was eager to discuss it with the business unit.

First contact with the business unit

Kristen had been working for the company for ten years, having joined the marketing department about five years earlier, and after holding various positions, now managed the department with significant success. She was ambitious and successful and wouldn't accept 'no' or 'impossible' for an answer. She battled to reach her goals and expectations and usually hit her targets.

Hakan knew Kristen well and had worked with her on numerous projects. He was aware of how important speed and flexibility were to her and so also knew that these concerns would be pivotal in convincing her to try Scrum.

Hakan called her to request a brief meeting about the CRM project. The project start date was approaching, and he told her that he had a new idea that he wanted to share with her, one that would guarantee the project's success.

Because the project's success was extremely important to her, getting Kristen on board took little persuasion. She was pleased to see that Hakan was prioritizing the project and that he had proposed the idea before the project had even begun. As they hadn't been able to get together for a while, they decided to meet for lunch to discuss the proposal.

In preparation for his meeting, Hakan reviewed his presentation with Mei. He planned to highlight examples and figures relating to the potential benefits of Scrum, rather than going into detail about what it entailed. Because results, speed, and flexibility were key considerations for Kristen, they could be used to help sell the concept to her.

They met for lunch in the canteen, and Kristen seemed a bit preoccupied. She had a busy day ahead, so they chatted a bit about day-to-day matters and touched on some personal issues before she moved the conversation to work.

There were several issues relating to projects that they had been working on, and she felt that he could help her resolve them. Hakan listened in silence, obligingly taking notes and promising to talk them through with the relevant project managers so that he could get back to her with some answers. Kristen seemed satisfied and said, "So, what did you want to discuss with me? As you know, the CRM project is very important to me, and I'm really glad to see that you're already working on it. What do you have in mind?"

Hakan had prepared some of the data that he had used in the presentation for Mei and gave examples of outcomes related to Scrum success cases. Without wasting more time, he laid the printouts on the table: "Kristen, as you know, speed and flexibility are essential in our projects; most projects are behind schedule and often incomplete. You're waiting for the project to finish before making important changes, and afterwards, you have to make sure that IT prioritizes these change requests and reserve a capacity to handle them. These situations create a serious burden on you, the IT unit, and obviously on us."

"Then tell the IT department to do their job properly!" Kristen responded. Hakan brushed her off and continued: "Unfortunately, these problems occur both in your department and on the software side, and it's the company itself that suffers most.

Recently, I've been reading about how other companies overcome similar problems, and one new approach in particular, called Scrum, seems very promising; it's very well regarded and has proven success." This didn't seem to impress Kristen, so Hakan knew that he had to share some quantitative facts in order to convince her. After providing examples from different international companies and projects that had used Scrum's flexibility and speed of time-to-market to their advantage, Kristen finally seemed interested.

Hakan explained the details of Scrum for nearly 15 minutes, with Kristen occasionally interjecting with quick questions and observations— "the sector that they operate in is quite different for implementing Scrum," she said. Time was running out, and Kristen had to leave for a meeting. She still wasn't fully convinced, but if the improvements were really possible, then she was open to persuasion:

"Hakan, as you know, using time effectively is my top priority. I would definitely like to complete projects faster, work more efficiently, and increase our flexibility. I don't care whether we use Scrum or any other methodology, I just want to see results. If you really believe that Scrum could help, then we need to discuss it in more detail. We can certainly give it a try— after all, it's not going to be worse than the current situation."

Hakan felt uncomfortable about Kristen blaming the PMO and IT department for all of the existing problems, but ultimately, he had succeeded in convincing her to try Scrum. They arranged to meet again to continue discussing the finer points of the process.

Convincing the IT department

Feeling hopeful, Hakan left the meeting with Kristen and went straight to Kieran, who, as usual, was tired and busy. "Kieran, I've found something more fun to save you from this situation!" Hakan exclaimed. But Kieran was unresponsive. "Have you heard about Scrum? I think we should try it in the CRM project." Kieran suddenly stopped what he was doing and asked excitedly, "Scrum? Really?"

"Yes, I've been working on Scrum recently, and I think we should implement it as soon as possible. I even talked to Mei about it. She was positive about experimenting with it on a project. I also talked to Kristen about using it on the CRM project. We haven't been able to talk in detail yet, but I think we can convince her." Kieran was enthusiastic: "This is great news! Some of my friends on the team have been looking at Scrum, too! We'd really like to do this kind of project. Evan is really interested in it, and we've had several discussions about applying Scrum in our projects. I think we should talk to Evan about this now. I'm sure he will be as excited as I am."

Hakan was taken aback by Kieran's uncustomary enthusiasm. He had imagined that the IT department would be easier to convince than the business unit, but he had no idea that they would not only be familiar with Scrum, but keen to try it. They decided to go straight to Evan.

A clear visionary with strong principles, Evan had been head of IT for two years, and he was generally moderate and well-respected by his team. It wouldn't be too hard to convince him of the need to apply Scrum.

Surprised to find Hakan and Kieran standing in front of him, Evan immediately assumed that there was a problem with one of the projects: "Hi guys, what's the issue now?"

Kieran jumped in, explaining that Hakan had come to him to get his opinion on using Scrum in the CRM project. Evan was visibly surprised; he generally perceived the PMO as a department that would be reluctant to relinquish control and embrace change. As Scrum would reduce the overall control of the PMO, Evan was stunned that the suggestion was coming from them. Having already discussed Scrum with his team, Evan had anticipated that the PMO would be resistant to the idea of using the Scrum framework and had been wondering how best to introduce it to them.

Hakan discussed the developmental stage and history of the idea to try Scrum in the company and also shared the outcome of recent meetings with Mei and Kristen. Kieran and Evan were keen to hear what he had to say, and Hakan was delighted to see that they shared his excitement. He went on to discuss his plans, not only for the first pilot project, but also for the future. Evan was relieved to find that Hakan fully understood the principles of Scrum and the impact it would have upon everyone involved.

"Well, let's say we convinced the business unit and decided to implement Scrum on this project. What would be your role?" Evan asked excitedly. Hakan's answer was simple: "I'm thinking of becoming the Scrum Master. Yes, I know that the team should select their own Scrum Master. What I'm trying to say is that I would like to take this role if it's okay with the team. I really want to be part of this and experience the change." This was not the response that Evan and Kieran expected. In previous conversations, they had considered the possibility of assigning the role to a specialized software developer or team leader. They had anticipated reluctance on the part of the PMO to accept the changes that Scrum would have on their department. Scrum was all about self-organization and teamwork, so the need for a project manager on Scrum projects would be removed. The existing structure of the organization was dependent on project managers, which would no longer be the case. They had tried to find solutions to this perceived barrier, as the PMO could not be expected to accept the relinquishment of their traditional responsibilities. In their earlier talks, Evan and his team had decided to suggest a reduced role for the PMO in Scrum projects. They would not be able to interfere with the team's self-organization and the practice of Scrum but would be kept up to date with the progress of the project. The Scrum Team[3] could request help from the PMO, as and when necessary, particularly on matters of organization and processes that were unfamiliar to the IT department, but the project manager would not be allowed to run the team. In foreseeing objections to Scrum from the PMO, they had expected challenges which now appeared not to be the case at all. Their greatest adversary had become their ally.

Evan responded to his proposal: "Actually, Hakan, my team and I have been talking about Scrum and thinking of practicing it in our work for quite a while now, and we're really keen to get started. To be quite honest, we thought that you would resist Scrum, since there is no project management role within the framework. So I'm a bit surprised that you've come to us with this suggestion. We really think that Scrum will bring significant benefits to some of our projects. It's absolutely vital that we reach agreement and cooperate effectively so that together, we can advance this change in such a way that the company benefits at the

---

[3] *The Scrum Team: The team consisting of Scrum Master, Product Owner, and Development Team.*

highest level."

Hakan was relieved. Instead of having to convince the IT department, he suddenly found them to be defenders of change. Evan's popularity with the company's business units would be a great help in introducing Scrum and driving the process. Evan continued, "So, what's your plan from here? Scrum can be used in the CRM project. We're ready to do what it takes. How should we proceed?" Hakan felt that for the time being, it was enough to know that they were willing and ready. He would have to relay his positive meetings with the business unit and IT department to Mei. He believed that she would be encouraged by the support of both parties and would approve experimenting with Scrum. He would then organize a meeting with all parties in order to officially approve the pilot project.

It had been an amazing day for Hakan. After positive meetings with Kristen, Evan, and Kieran, he couldn't wait to share his news with Mei. There had been very little resistance up to this point, and he knew he had to act fast to direct the wind of change within the company. He thanked Evan and Kieran for taking the time to hear what he had to say and for supporting Scrum's implementation. He promised to get back to them with more details as soon as possible.

After Hakan left, Evan and Kieran shared their astonishment at this sudden turn of events. Evan wanted to discuss the issue of designating the role of Scrum Master: "How do you feel about Hakan being the Scrum Master, rather than one of us?"

Kieran had given this some thought during the meeting:

"Well, we were afraid that the project manager wouldn't understand the concept of Scrum and would therefore interfere with the team, so we never considered that possibility. Now it seems that Hakan is more convinced and enthusiastic about the need for Scrum than many of our friends in the department. You know, I've worked with him before, he's an experienced and competent person. I'd also say that he's a good leader, and we usually get along well. He's reasonable and understanding and always does his best to help us. When I think about it, why shouldn't he prove himself as the Scrum Master on this project?"

Both Evan and Kieran agreed that since the suggestion had come from the PMO, specifically from Hakan, it would be sensible and diplomatic to accept him as Scrum Master. The support of the PMO would be a great help in implementing and proving the benefits of Scrum. They were still stunned that, contrary to their expectations, the PMO would be a help, rather than a hindrance, in putting these new principles into action.

It all seemed very positive, but they were quite aware that there was a long road ahead, and they would have to proceed cautiously, as change of this magnitude was inherently unpredictable.

The green light for Scrum

Hakan went to Mei with news of his meetings, the enthusiastic response of the IT department, and Kristen's support for his proposal. Mei was surprised to hear that he had managed to make such rapid progress. His commitment to Scrum was clear, and he was working very hard to make it happen. Winning the support of the relevant parties was testament to his firm belief in the power of Scrum to bring progressive change to all.

There were so many positive indicators that Mei couldn't see any reason why they shouldn't trial Scrum on the CRM project, as Hakan suggested. If everyone else shared this commitment to making it work, it would be unreasonable to deny him the opportunity to prove it and thereby lose the potential for better working practices and more positive outcomes for the company. Mei was happy to give the green light for Scrum to proceed.

Hakan had several more meetings with Evan to work out the details of Scrum's implementation. Though there were some minor initial disagreements, they were able to resolve them through healthy negotiation. They were all eager to begin work on the project, but they had yet to receive full approval from the business unit.

Hakan managed to have brief meetings with Kristen and Johanna, the member of Kristen's team responsible for the CRM project. Kristen and Johanna were unconcerned about the finer details, as they could see that the PMO and the IT team were enthusiastic and committed to Scrum. Their primary concern was to complete the project and see results as soon as possible. The only issue they had was with the need for a 'Product Owner,'[4] a role

---
[4] *Product Owner: The person accountable for optimizing the value a product delivers, primarily by managing and expressing product functions and solutions in a Product Backlog. The single representative of all stakeholders and consumers.*

they would have to take on. They were already overstretched and weren't keen to assume any further responsibilities.

In order to overcome their resistance, Hakan explained the purpose of the role, clarifying how it would add value to the project. After all, the project was theirs, and it didn't seem reasonable to expect the results they wanted without taking an active role. It was an important project for them, and their participation was essential in directing the scope to achieve success, which was only possible if the software team and the business unit worked together. Cohesion was a vital part of the Scrum process.

Reluctant to devote even more of her time to the project, Johanna was resistant to taking on the role, but Kristen agreed that the request seemed reasonable and gave her full support to Hakan. She could see that taking an active role in delivering the project was necessary in order for the project to succeed, which was the top priority. The project was too important to be left unsupervised and would need to be closely monitored. Kristen's agreement on this final point meant that Hakan would be able to begin the pilot project and ultimately prove Scrum's worth.

Progress had been much faster than Hakan had anticipated, having taken less than a month to reach the threshold of change. He recognized the need to maintain momentum and begin the project as soon as possible.

Chapter II:
Let the Change Begin!

Transformation Action List[5]

Finally, everything was ready: a pilot project, a team willing to implement Scrum, and convinced executives. Everything was about to change for Hakan and the team. Having already succeeded in persuading managers and the team to practice Scrum, Hakan hadn't thought about what to do next. But after working tirelessly for months to get to this point, Hakan had gained the confidence he needed to begin implementing the Scrum model.

At the previous meeting, the decision was made to start the project within a matter of weeks. Hakan and his team had to begin preparations as soon as possible. In order to be able to lead the change, he needed to formulate a rough plan. This high-level plan would include some major steps to guide the implementation of Scrum on the pilot project and, after having proven success with the pilot project, initiate more profound change within the company. These action items would enable him to oversee the daily running of the process without getting lost in the details, allowing him to provide direction and pre-empt any problems .

He listed a few actions: firstly, the team would have to be taught the Scrum principles, as they had never worked with them before. They needed to understand the significant changes that Scrum would require and be prepared to work according to the new framework. After the training, the team had to come together, clarify some ground rules around how they would implement the Scrum framework, organize the handover of their current ongoing duties so that they could focus on their new project, and make the necessary technical preparations. Finding an appropriate designated workspace for the team would be another priority.

---

[5] *Transformation Action List: A list of items that should be acted on to ensure successful implementation and widespread use of Scrum.*

Their first challenge was to form a productive team; in order to create the necessary cohesion, they all had to be involved in preparations from the outset. The preparation process would be an opportunity for Hakan to observe the team and identify potential obstacles and points of resistance to change. To complete these preparations, they could begin the first studies immediately after the training period, with a kick-off process that would last for a few weeks at most.

The next stage was to finish the kick-off process and start the first Sprint[6] immediately afterwards. Afterwards, they would proceed within the framework of the 'Inspect and Adapt' principle. Having started the first Sprint, Hakan had to have a rough plan, with guidelines on how to steer change. At this point, change should proceed in two fundamentally interconnected areas. One of them was a change in the way the team delivered the value and the angle from which they would approach the project. The other was a more radical change that would capitalize on the strength of the team having successfully implemented previous changes, which would then precipitate a transformation in company culture. To allow for such transformation, the team had to deliver successful business results on the pilot project. The team's understanding of the Scrum process, as well as Hakan's ability to guide and support them in their endeavors, was essential in achieving the overall outcome he hoped for.

In order to attain success, the team first had to acquire the basic Scrum reflex. They had to learn to be a team, to self-organize, and to create transparency. Depending on these factors, a certain quality and delivery cadence could be achieved, and they would begin to produce an outcome that would satisfy the

---

[6] *Sprint: An event that serves as a container for the other Scrum events, time-boxed to four weeks or less. The event serves getting a sufficient amount of work done, while ensuring timely inspection, reflection and adaptation at a product and strategic level. The other Scrum events are Sprint Planning, Daily Scrum, Sprint Review, and Sprint Retrospective.*

customer in every Sprint. After these reflexes were formed, they could then focus on productivity and continue working on creating Kaizen[7] culture. Parallel with this, Hakan had to communicate and promote change outside of the existing team to trigger a bigger change within the company; this would be far more challenging than implementing Scrum on the pilot project.

Hakan would keep all the stakeholders and managers involved in the pilot project informed about Scrum processes and objectives. He would have to communicate with managers about the goals they aimed to achieve on this project and the support that they would need. Working alongside the Product Owner, he would invite them to the Sprint Review[8] events and keep them closely involved in the process so that the team's achievements would be evident and any help that they needed would be on hand. There was no doubt that more extensive support would be needed for broad and fundamental change.

Keeping the decision-making mechanisms of the company informed about and receptive to Scrum and the success achieved on the pilot project was vital. Increasing awareness and attracting the attention of managers would ensure the expansion of change.

With these actions in place, Hakan was ready to begin executing the next steps. There would be alterations and adjustments during the journey, but for now, planning the training was his priority.

---

[7] *Kaizen: Change for a better, continuous improvement mindset. (Japanese "kai": change, "zen": good, better).*
[8] *Sprint Review Event: An event marking the closing of the development of a Sprint, time-boxed to four hours or less. The event serves for the Scrum Team and the stakeholders to inspect the Increment, the overall progress and strategic changes in order to allow the Product Owner to update the Product Backlog.*

TRANSFORMATION ACTION LIST

TARGET	ACTION
Start pilot project	Scrum Training for the team
Start pilot project	Team kickoff and handling preparations
Start pilot project	Start the first Sprint
Attract attention and create interest in change	Introductory session for the management and stakeholders about Scrum and its new way of working
Attract attention and create interest in change	Stakeholder involvement in the process
Attract attention and create interest in change	Company-wide short, introductory awareness sessions about Scrum
Establish Scrum Reflex	Getting the team used to working with the Scrum framework, facilitate Scrum events
Establish Scrum Reflex	Form team norms
Establish Scrum Reflex	Enhance transparency
Establish Scrum Reflex	Enhance teamwork
Establish Scrum Reflex	Support self-organization behavior
Trigger Kaizen Culture	?

Kick-off

The team had completed the training and knew what to expect of Scrum in the coming days. Bored with the monotony of their old work method, they were inspired by the prospect of Scrum and were impatient to start the project. Aware of their excitement, right after the training, Hakan brought the team together to answer their questions and talk about how to begin.

Though the meeting was scheduled to begin at 10 a.m., Hakan was still waiting for everyone to arrive. Old habits were hard to break; punctuality was not a feature of their working practice, and they were unaccustomed to meetings beginning on time. There was even a conception among colleagues that if you were punctual, you had too much time on your hands and obviously weren't busy enough. Clearly, changing behaviors was going to be a challenge for Hakan.

Once everyone had arrived, Hakan calmly asked the team to shut down their computers and focus on the meeting, but no one seemed to respond, so he repeated his request with a more serious tone. Looking up from his work, Michael said: "I have an important task I need to take care of right now, unfortunately. I can't turn off my computer, but don't worry, I'm listening to you." The others nodded in agreement.

Hakan responded, maintaining his composure: "Guys, I understand, but we're already starting late. We don't have much time, and we need to make some quick decisions, so you need to forget about other things now and focus on this meeting. The decisions we make here will directly affect you. You are the owners of this project, and you should leave other tasks and concentrate for the next half hour. If there are people waiting for your response, please let them know that you are busy right now, and you'll get back to them right after the meeting."

He was struggling already; what had happened to the enthusiasm of the team over the last few weeks? They had seemed so eager before but didn't appear to be sharing his excitement now. With the struggle to begin meetings on time, the team trying to multi-task when they should be focused, and the fact that they were still expected to deal with other ongoing tasks, Hakan's challenges were clearer already. He would have his work cut out for him.

Michael reluctantly turned off his computer and began speaking: "You're right Hakan, we do need to focus on this. Obviously I want to do that, but what about other commitments? Tasks from other projects are still being assigned to me. Should I refuse them? How do I explain this?" Hakan responded: "Michael, I totally understand. Actually, this is one of the reasons for the meeting. How about I explain why we're here and what we're trying to do, and then we can discuss your issue?" Michael reluctantly agreed.

Hakan explained that before starting their Sprints, they would begin with a short setup for relevant preparations. They had to keep this setup period as short as possible so that they could begin their first Sprint.

He asked them to think about what they should do to be ready and able to produce a working piece of software, beginning with their very first Sprint. The preparations they made here would be the first priority items of their Product Backlog[9]. To help the team, Hakan asked them to think about the Scrum

---

[9] *Product Backlog: An ordered, evolving list of all work deemed necessary by the Product Owner to create, deliver, maintain, and sustain a product.*

framework and its attributes: "Are our Scrum roles defined? Johanna is the Product Owner, and you are the Development Team. What about our Scrum Master? Honestly, I have volunteered for the Scrum Master role, but it is up to your decision."

The team discussed the role and quickly decided that Hakan was the best fit. After all, he was the most knowledgeable about Scrum among the team.

Hakan continued to ask the team about the remaining attributes of the Scrum framework, like the Sprint length, for example. As he continued to write on the whiteboard, the team began to get involved with suggestions of their own.

After a short time, the team had established the necessary preparation actions and decisions they needed to make:

- Sprint Length
- Event Schedule
    - Daily Scrum[10]
    - Sprint Planning [11]
    - Sprint Review
    - Sprint Retrospective[12]

- Creating the initial Product Backlog
- Creating the Definition of Done[13]

---

[10] *Daily Scrum: A daily event, time-boxed to 15 minutes or less, to re-plan the development work during a Sprint. The event serves for the Development Team to share the daily progress, plan the work for the next 24 hours and update the Sprint Backlog accordingly.*

[11] *Sprint Planning Event: An event marking the start of a Sprint, time-boxed to eight hours or less. The event serves for the Scrum Team to inspect the Product Backlog considered most valuable at that time and design that forecast into an initial Sprint Backlog against the Sprint Goal.*

[12] *Sprint Retrospective Event: An event marking the closing of a Sprint, time-boxed to three hours or less. The event serves for the Scrum Team to inspect the Sprint that is ending and establish the way of working for the next Sprint.*

[13] *Definition of Done: The set of expectations on quality that a product Increment must exhibit to make it releasable, i.e. fit for a release to the product's users.*

- Arrangements for a team room
- Creating the Scrum Board[14]
- Handing over ongoing tasks which are not part of the new project
- System installation and technical setup
- Deciding when to finalize decisions on the previous items and realize them so that they can begin Sprint 1.

There was more to do than Hakan had thought, but they were almost at the end of the timebox[15] set for the meeting, and they still hadn't thoroughly discussed the actions. This was a warning for Hakan and the team. They were not yet a tight unit, and there were many new concepts to consider, so it took time for them to decide on any issue. When determining timeboxes for future meetings, this should be taken into account. The team decided to finish the meeting in accordance with the timebox and meet again at 3 p.m. for a two-hour time slot. He had one more question before everyone left the room: could everyone arrive on time?! The team agreed that they would be on time and there was no need to worry. He hoped that they would do as promised.

The team slowly began trickling in around 3 p.m., and Hakan was pleased to see that this time, there were no laptops. The morning wake-up call had been effective, and he proudly waited for all of the team members to arrive. When the meeting began not long after the scheduled time, he briefly reminded the team of the purpose of the meeting: to establish the duration need for setup and goals they aimed to achieve within this timebox. There was much to discuss, so they immediately began to review the action items.

---

[14] *Sprint Backlog (Scrum Board): An evolving plan of all work deemed necessary by the Development Team to realize a Sprint's goal. Mostly represented via the Scrum Board.*

[15] *Timebox: A container in time of a maximum duration, potentially a fixed duration. In Scrum, all events have a maximum duration only, except for the Sprint itself, which has a fixed duration.*

Hakan was pleased that the meeting progressed without too much intervention on his part, and he was satisfied with the team's cooperation and the discussions that ensued. Some decisions were made quickly, while others involved intense debate. One such debate involved specifying the Sprint duration. Cautious members wanted to have a longer Sprint length to be on the safe side, while others, wanting increased flexibility and quicker results, argued for a shorter timescale. As the team seemed stuck on this issue, Hakan briefly intervened, postponing the decision and encouraging them to continue with other issues. By delaying the decision on the contentious issue of the Sprint length, he took the pressure off the timebox and restored team harmony, resulting in agreement on other issues.

Throughout the meeting, Hakan observed the team: Kieran and Alex were experienced software developers, experts in their field, and enthusiastic about Scrum. During the discussions, they were moderate and supportive; they were clearly invested in the success of the project. Michael was the team's business analyst, one of the best in the company. He was also enthusiastic but obviously didn't believe that some things could change; his resistance was apparent. Sarah was the last member of the Scrum Development Team[16], having joined the testing team about two years previously. Hakan noticed that Sarah hadn't contributed much until now but had quietly adapted to the team and its decisions. Johanna, the Product Owner, though clearly articulating her excitement for the project and Scrum, seemed a bit bored of the meeting. Hakan guessed that she wasn't keen to be too involved with this aspect of the process.

Before Sprint 1 began, Hakan's list of challenges was growing. These included arranging a team room, helping the team learn

---

[16] *Development Team: The group of people accountable for all evolutionary development work needed to create a releasable Increment no later than by the end of a Sprint.*

to work together, dealing with Johanna's perceived separation from the team, and Michael's resistance to change.

The end of the meeting was imminent, but many issues were discussed and agreed upon. After taking a short break and revisiting the Sprint length issue, the team was able to set the time frame at two weeks. The setup period would take the same amount of time as the Sprint. In the meantime, they would hand over the work and finish their preparations so that they could fully focus on Sprint 1.

One decision was not yet made—the team name—and Hakan felt that it was important in uniting the team and helping them feel connected. There were a few suggestions, but none felt right. So they decided to rethink the name later and added it to their list.

The timely commencement of the meeting meant that it ended efficiently, according to the timebox. Hakan was delighted with the team members' cooperation and contributions. Despite a few issues, they had set their goals and had begun to learn to work together.

Preparation Actions	Acceptance Criteria
Create initial Product Backlog	Enough items to cover at least a few upcoming Sprints
Estimation?	Get poker planning cards
Get a team room	Reserve a dedicated working room for the team
Team room setup	Establish the team name, Scrum Board, and Sprint Burndown Chart[17]
Definition of Done	Place it in the room visible to everyone
Handing over ongoing tasks from other projects	Zero assigned work remaining

---

[17] *Sprint Burndown Chart: A chart showing the decrease of remaining work against time.*

The team room

Finding a place to hold a meeting was always a challenge, with everyone competing for rooms. It seemed almost impossible to find a permanent room for the Development Team to work comfortably together around the same table throughout the project, which would be necessary in maintaining team spirit. Hakan had a look at some of the IT meeting rooms, but though some seemed suitable, they were also the most frequently requested by other members of the department. Reserving them for 8-9 months would not be an option. He had been offered the use of two rooms, but neither would be appropriate, as they were both too small, one being in the sub-basement, and the other, depressingly windowless; the team was not happy.

As Scrum Master, Hakan had to find a better option, since successfully solving this problem would increase the team's confidence in him. He also knew how important it was for team morale and motivation for them to feel that they were valued as the first team to trial Scrum. Sprint 1 had not even begun, and he had a mountain of problems to deal with. But he had no intention of giving up. These obstacles would not deter him from his goal.

Hakan decided to enlist Evan's help, as he was as invested in Scrum as he was. If he could get Evan on board, they might be able to get one of the rooms that the team favored.

Evan welcomed him warmly, asking if the project had begun and whether things were going well. After discussing the kick-off event, meeting outcomes, goals, and the team's confidence in the project, Evan seemed pleased.

Hakan also discussed their problems, including the ongoing non-project-related tasks and the stress that these issues were causing. Hakan and the team needed Evan's help to solve these problems. Evan listened carefully and took notes on relevant issues that he could address to ease the burden on Hakan and the team. He was determined to give them his full support, as he firmly believed in the importance of the project. He reiterated that he was always available to help with anything he could.

When Hakan came to the tricky issue of finding the right team room, Evan suggested two of the rooms that had already been offered to them, obviously not realizing that they were inadequate and would demotivate them. He was worried that Evan would say, "These are the best alternatives we have. Unfortunately, we have to deal with it." But he didn't. Instead, he said that though he thought that his suggested options complied with their requirements, he would be happy to help secure the best room available if they were unsuitable. Hakan was relieved that Evan understood the importance of finding the right base and was surprised by his ready offer of support. He mentioned the two preferred rooms, and Evan immediately offered to speak with the people in charge about giving one of them to Hakan as soon as possible. The most important issue was time. The team had started preparations without a dedicated workspace, and Evan, aware of the urgency and importance of the situation, said that he would get back to him with a solution by the following day.

Hakan was immensely relieved and buoyantly left Evan's room. From the outset, he had valued Evan's positive involvement in the Scrum process. Evan's backing was pivotal, and thanks to him, Hakan no longer had to worry about the team room and now could focus on other preparation items.

An unhelpful practice: handing over ongoing tasks

The team was preparing to start, but the process of handing over non-project tasks was not going as smoothly or speedily as desired. The problems centered around Michael. Michael's manager, David, acknowledged that Michael's main task was to work with the Scrum team, but he didn't want Michael to focus solely on that project. Michael was an expert in his field; his absence from other projects could pose a serious risk to David's output, so Hakan would have his work cut out for him in convincing David that the Scrum team needed Michael's total commitment.

Hakan went to David to explain the importance of the pilot project for the company as a whole and stressed that all team members had to be focused on the project to ensure that it progressed effectively and successfully. David was unconvinced; there were a lot of important projects running within the company, and total dedication to just one of them was impossible. Besides, Michael was a talented business analyst, and David believed that he could easily support other business alongside this work. He couldn't see any reason why Michael should be expected to stop working on other projects just because he was involved in Scrum.

It was clear that Hakan would not be able to convince David to change his mind. David didn't understand the Scrum framework and the need for total focus to ensure effectiveness and prevent the process from descending into chaos. His only option would be to try and support Michael and encourage him to prioritize their pilot project and commit to the team as much as possible, contrary to David's wishes.

David's resistance could have been about Scrum, or about the idea of change itself. Maybe the loss of one of his crew made him feel like he was losing authority. All of the managers within the company competed to increase the number of teams they were responsible for in order to strengthen their position. On the other hand, since David's priority was to ensure that all of his projects were successful, he could be concerned that losing months of Michael's time would greatly affect his performance and targets. Or maybe he just didn't think that the current structure needed to be changed.

Hakan couldn't be sure of the exact reasons for David's resistance, but it was clear that taking a hard stand against him would be pointless. Insisting that Michael committed solely to the pilot project against his manager's wishes could seriously damage the project. For now, he had to manage the situation carefully. He placated David, letting him know that he understood his position but hoped that he would nevertheless support the Scrum pilot project. Hakan kindly asked him to ensure that Michael's work on other projects would not compromise his responsibility to this one. David assured him that he needn't have doubts. The success of the pilot project, like any other project, was also important to his team, and as always, they would do their part. They concluded the meeting by agreeing that after a few Sprints, Michael's involvement in other projects outside of Scrum would be gradually reduced. Nevertheless, Hakan was well aware that David, despite his assurances, would never allow Michael to totally disengage from other projects.

Hakan seemed to have conceded his first loss; creating a focused team able to fully experience the Scrum way of working seemed impossible. However, he was comforted by the fact that instigating change was a process and that things would not always go entirely according to plan. As the project progressed and proved its merits, his position would be strengthened, allowing him greater influence within the company. The transparency of Scrum would clearly demonstrate factors affecting productivity, and the supporting data would confirm the need to change habits and conform to Scrum good practices in order to increase performance. Though the first Sprint would not have a totally dedicated team, Michael's help would be invaluable in accelerating the delivery of value.

Closing the preparations

It was time to examine the results of the actions that the team had planned in readiness for the first Sprint, and almost everyone was in the team room on time. They quickly began to run through their preparation actions.

The Development Team worked together with Johanna to form the Product Backlog. Fibonacci numbers were selected as the estimation system, and they had estimated the relative size of most of the user stories in the initial Product Backlog. A list of priorities was set alongside these items and estimations. The top ranked items for the first 3-4 Sprints were particularly clear and detailed enough to enable them to smoothly progress through the Backlog.

Though it had taken some time, arrangements for the team room were also complete, and everyone was pleased with the results of Hakan's efforts. His commitment and willingness to help them find an appropriate working space had increased their respect and confidence in him. After settling on 'A-Team' as their official team name, they had proudly hung a poster-sized team logo on the wall next to the Scrum Board and Sprint Burndown Chart. To boost company awareness, they had also placed a small team logo on the door. The scope of 'Done' had been defined, framed, and hung on the inside of the door to remind them of their working standards every time they left the room. The reminder would help them to maintain quality and prompt them to follow up on the remaining work during the Sprint progress.

The only issue was that the Development Team had not yet allocated non-project-related tasks to other teams. Apart from

Michael, most of the team had made more time to work on the project, but ultimately, no one was able to transfer all of their other tasks, which made some team members uncomfortable. From the outset, Michael had felt that this would be an impossible feat. Although Hakan seemed to have initially convinced Michael and the team to transfer their non-project-related tasks so that they could focus on the project, no one had succeeded in accomplishing this over the last two weeks. The worst thing was that new tasks were still coming in.

Hakan immediately recognized the problem with the team's confidence in focusing on the new project. It wasn't surprising that the team was unmotivated, but he wouldn't give up. He explained to the team that this was a process of change, and that in a few Sprints time, it would all come together. The team shouldn't give up hope. On the contrary, they should increase their efforts to prove how critical focus was to the project. Apart from the problems with Michael, everything seemed to be going fairly well. After a few Sprints, the other members of the team would most likely resolve the dedication issue; however, it was apparent that they had to plan clearer and more radical steps to solve this problem.

This meeting was perhaps not the best place to discuss problems and seek solutions. On the other hand, the subjects for discussion were nearly complete, sooner than they had expected, and the timebox had about an hour remaining. So Hakan took the opportunity to discuss the problem of Michael's multiple responsibilities. The team agreed that this was an important matter because for the team to succeed, it was crucial that everyone had the time to focus solely on the project. And at least for the meantime, Michael's role was especially critical.

They discussed the obstacles Michael faced in enabling him to hand over his tasks. In fact, the issue was simple: Michael didn't know to whom to allocate these tasks. Since David hadn't yet decided on how to resolve this, they had to choose the person, or people, to whom Michael could complete the handover, which needed to be done as soon as possible. Michael said that if needed, he was willing to work overtime, but Hakan wasn't happy with that solution. Somehow, they should be able to succeed and cooperate as a team within normal working hours.

The team agreed to work with Hakan during the first Sprint to decide on whom Michael could transfer his tasks to. As a first step, Hakan and Michael were keen to meet with David. If they couldn't get his support, Michael would meet with his close peers in order to find a solution. Hakan would also ask Evan and Mei for their input. The aim of their next Sprint would be to decide on who could assume Michael's non-project-related tasks.

The team added this issue to their Product Backlog. The meeting had progressed quickly and effectively, and Hakan was pleased with the team's ownership of their actions. They had reached the meeting goals in half of the predicted timebox and had demonstrated their ability to identify problems and produce solutions. These were positive signs that team spirit was being formed. Still, the team had a long road ahead in achieving the goal of Kaizen culture. Hakan would have to be patient and follow the team closely during the process, since he understood that this positive momentum could reverse unexpectedly, and at any time.

Hakan's other concern was Johanna's reticence in participating in the meeting. He perceived that she didn't feel that her contribution was necessary, though she hadn't explicitly said it or complained about being there. He knew that before this became an issue, he had to make her feel like a valued member of the team. Unfortunately, there wasn't much that he could do at the moment. All he could do now was try to stay as close as possible to her by helping her work on the Product Backlog during the first Sprint. Hakan hoped that by the time it was over, the team would be more involved in the process and could own the project as they produced the increments.

SPRINT 1: THE FIRST SPRINT PLANNING

Before the meeting began, Johanna asked Hakan if it would be a problem if she missed the meeting, as she had a more urgent one to attend. After all, she said, they had already discussed the user stories in detail a few days ago, so the team could now address the items in order of priority and begin the Sprint. This confirmed Hakan's observations about Johanna during the setup period. She was obviously not yet ready to adopt the process and clearly didn't see herself as part of the team. Therefore, Hakan wasn't surprised that she was trying to excuse herself from the first meeting. He responded that she must attend the Sprint Planning event. Yes, they had already worked on the Product Backlog, so the meeting wouldn't take too long, but in order to respond to questions that may arise during the meeting, and most importantly, to set the goal of the Sprint together with the team, she had to be there. He asked her to delay her other meeting, and Johanna had little choice but to comply with his request.

They walked towards the team room together, as there were only a few minutes left before the event was due to start. The other members of the team were not yet there, and Hakan was worried that the event would not begin on time, which would give the already reluctant Johanna a reason to excuse herself for her other meeting. He was just about to call the team when they began to arrive. He was relieved, but also angry with himself for not trusting them to be punctual. The team took their places slowly, but their excitement was evident.

Hakan began by reminding the team of the purpose and

structure of the Sprint Planning event, and the meeting began on a positive note. Johanna discussed her objective for the first Sprint and moved forward with prioritized items while answering occasional questions from the team. Prompted by these questions, they divided several user stories into smaller slices and added some new technical stories to the Product Backlog. Hakan hoped that this would convince Johanna that the attendance of all team members, including her, was crucial.

Later, the team began to argue once again about some size estimates they had already made. They obviously didn't yet feel comfortable about this new estimation technique. During their discussion, many members tried to create a time reference, with comments like "this item is a half-day job." Hakan occasionally intervened, asking the team to forget about the time and instead try to make a relative estimation. He also reminded them that after a few Sprints, making size estimates independent of time would be easier. As work began, they would be better able to estimate the magnitude of the items and learn to move through the Fibonacci Numbers relatively easily. It was just a matter of time.

The team had made some changes in size estimates, albeit with a bit of difficulty, but there was another important issue that Hakan had noted during the meeting — Sarah had rarely spoken. Although she had quietly listened to the team's discussions and was agreeable with their suggestions, she appeared reluctant to share her own views. Hakan felt that this was not due to any weakness on her part, or a resistance to Scrum, but that she was just a bit reticent and perhaps shy by nature. He believed that as the process evolved, she would become more confident and therefore participate more actively in discussions. To speed up this process, he could encourage her to speak more, but he felt that it was still too early for that. He would give her a bit more time to settle in rather than forcing the issue.

It had been about two hours since they had begun, and the Development Team had decided on which top-ranked user stories they could pull for the first Sprint. Johanna agreed with their decisions—the first Sprint Goal[18] was clear to everyone. Johanna could now leave the event and, after a short break, the Development Team would create a general Sprint plan by elaborating on the stories they forecasted completing in order to reach the Sprint Goal. After the break, Hakan reminded the team to divide each story[19] into a to-do-list like tasks and to prepare the Scrum Board. They still had nearly two hours before the end of the timebox, so there was no pressure. At this point, it looked like everything was going to plan.

Hakan had no additional contributions to make, so he moved to the back of the room. The team was clearly able to continue planning the Sprint without his input, so he withdrew and left them to it. Turning on his laptop, he began reading his emails, still listening in on the discussion. Observing quietly, he would still be able to intervene in any difficult discussions and would also see how the team worked together. The Development Team began to break the stories down into smaller to-do tasks. They were sharing constructive ideas among themselves, while including Sarah, who had not spoken much until then but had now become actively involved in the debate.

The Scrum Board began to fill up with the Sprint Backlog Items, for which the team was able to quickly make time estimates. They seemed less confident, however, about estimating

---

[18] *Sprint Goal: A concise statement expressing the overarching purpose of a Sprint.*
[19] *Story/User Story: Product Backlog Item, a potential feature to be added to the product.*

timescales. Cautious team members suggested longer timescales, saying things like "let's make it a bit higher for the worst-case scenario." Hakan was hesitant to interfere; obviously the team was trying to cover itself. Because of old habits, they were used to exaggerating the numbers in order to make their estimates. During the Sprint, however, they would learn that time estimates on the Sprint Backlog Items were meant to help them approximate the remaining work for the Sprint; no one would judge if their time estimates weren't exact. For this reason, he chose not to intervene so that the team could arrive at this realization on their own. This would result in the new mindset that the team could learn through practice.

Half an hour before the timebox expired, the team was ready to end the event, as there didn't seem to be any remaining work to be done. They calculated the total time estimate for the to-do tasks they had created for the Sprint, which was close to the team's two-week Sprint capacity. Hakan thought this may pose a risk because it was highly probable that during this short meeting, the team would not be able to identify all of the related to-do tasks necessary to achieve their Sprint Goal. It was to be expected that they would discover additional tasks in order to make the stories 'Done' according to their defined standards. Because the team and the project were new, Hakan did not expect things to run perfectly during the first few Sprints.

According to Hakan, the team didn't seem to have made realistic time estimates for reassigning non-project-related tasks. On the other hand, he felt that they had made unnecessarily high predictions for other tasks. The two might balance each other out, Hakan thought. Still, the team seemed at more risk of struggling during this Sprint than they had anticipated.

Although Hakan had concerns, the team was pleased with their work, so he didn't interfere. They had to be able to identify and solve their problems and shortcomings on their own within the Sprint. He asked the team whether they were all clear about the Sprint Goal, as well as how to proceed with this objective. Since the team seemed confident that they were fully prepared, the event was brought to a close.

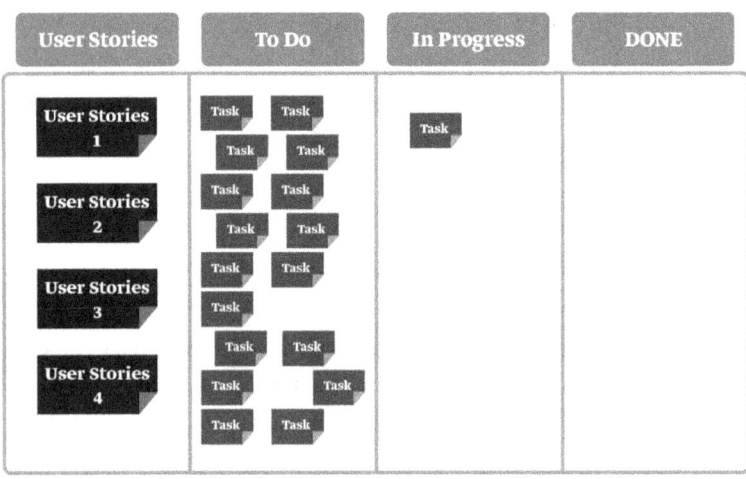

Scrum Board (includes the Product Backlog Items forecasted to be delivered in the actual Sprint, as well as tasks associated with each Item in order to make them Done)

First daily scrum

At their first Daily Scrum, Hakan arrived earlier than usual, filled with enthusiasm and anticipation. Would the team arrive on time? Would they follow the Daily Scrum's principles? What would the atmosphere be like? With almost an hour before the meeting, he decided to read over his notes to brush up on the Scrum Master's role during these events. It was good to be reminded of the importance of the passive role of the Scrum Master—that is, to refrain from taking too much initiative in order to ensure that the team was self-organizing. The purpose of the Daily Scrum was to enable the team to review their progress towards the Sprint Goal and trigger team spirit. As Scrum Master, Hakan's role was to create a conducive environment without much intervention or management.

> **Hakan's Notes to Himself About Daily Scrum:**
> - ✔ 3 questions for the team:
>   - *what did I do yesterday to meet the Sprint Goal?*
>   - *what will I do today to meet the Sprint Goal?*
>   - *are there any impediments in the way of achieving the Sprint Goal?*
> - ✔ This is not a reporting event, make the team feel safe
> - ✔ Let the team explore their progress towards the Sprint Goal
> - ✔ Be sure everybody speaks
> - ✔ Ensure that the board and the Burndown Chart have been updated

The team slowly trickled into the office. Everyone seemed happy and relaxed, having been able to leave on time the day before, which was rare. Other than that, it seemed like a normal day. They greeted Hakan, opened their laptops, and got to work. Hakan checked his watch; it was as if they had all forgotten about the Daily Scrum. He reminded them that the meeting would start in a few minutes, as he couldn't bear the suspense.

It seemed to be a useful reminder, as they all looked surprised before slowly gathering around him at the Scrum Board. He asked the team what they planned to do during the Daily Scrum, and whether they remembered its purpose. Since everyone seemed aware of the event's principles, Hakan stepped back and allowed Michael to speak. Michael talked about what he had already done and about his plan for the day, which was exactly what Hakan had hoped for. He finished by updating the Scrum Board with his progress and plans. Following Michael's lead, Kieran addressed Hakan as if he wanted his approval to continue, but Hakan encouraged him to address the group instead, as he didn't want to intervene or take a managerial role.

Each of the team members followed suit in offering their contributions to the meeting, but as nobody mentioned potential problems, Hakan asked if he could do anything to help. None were forthcoming; they all shook their heads, except Michael, who wanted to ask him about the task reassignment issue. They had identified the steps and tasks related to this issue during the planning meeting, and Hakan had agreed to help Michael through the process, so they arranged to get together after the meeting to discuss how to proceed.

During the Daily Scrum, the team made some changes to the Scrum Board, adding several new small tasks and changing the time estimates of some existing ones. They reflected these changes in the Sprint Burndown Chart, and the event was over.

Hakan was pleased that there were no serious problems. Minor improvements would happen over time, as the team became accustomed to this new way of working. In the meantime, he and Michael headed to the cafe to discuss the non-project-related tasks.

THE SCRUM MASTER'S OBSERVATIONS SO FAR

The first week of the Sprint was almost over, and the team was trying to progress according to their strategy created at the Sprint Planning event. However, they were not progressing as fast as they had planned, because in order to achieve the Sprint Goal, there was more work than they had initially anticipated. This was bad news for the team; they had a lot to do to complete the stories and not much time in which to do it. This seemed to affect their motivation, since it seemed impossible to achieve everything that the first Sprint required.

The Scrum Board and Sprint Burndown Chart clearly showed how much was yet to be achieved, and progress was very slow. The team appeared dispirited, frustrated, and worried that they would not succeed at their first Sprint. Hakan tried to reassure them that this was to be expected and that they shouldn't let it affect their motivation. Instead of worrying about delivering all the forecasted stories that they had pulled into their Sprint, they could instead focus on potential new strategies to achieve the Sprint Goal and deliver value.

Lack of planning wasn't the only issue facing the team; they were continually interrupted throughout the day, which they hadn't anticipated. These interruptions put them under great stress, knowing that success required their full focus. Hakan had anticipated that such interruptions would be a problem, but it was only through experiencing them in the context of the Sprint that the team was able to see the negative impact that these demands had on their work. They would all have to work hard to minimize such interruptions, since no one wanted to put the Sprint at risk—this was an important lesson for them to learn.

Although stressful, the challenges that the team was experiencing were having a positive effect on accelerating team formation. They were debating every challenge they faced, and Hakan felt that these discussions were constructive, as they provided an opportunity to establish teamwork norms. The team was consolidating by discussing problems and finding solutions, which was great to see during the first Sprint; all in all, Hakan was extremely satisfied with the way the team was developing.

Johanna's case, on the other hand, was slightly different, since she was swamped with her daily marketing tasks and couldn't find the necessary time to devote to the team. Hakan had been to see her several times to maintain communication, encourage her to be more involved in the process, and to help her work on the Product Backlog. Unfortunately, however, she hadn't had much time for such discussions and kept their meetings very brief. He was finding it hard to involve Johanna and see her as part of the team, but he knew it was important to stay calm and not pressure her. He was confident that when she attended the Sprint events and saw the fast-moving, productive team in action, she would realize that she needed to dedicate more time to the project to help the team succeed.

In order to deepen his knowledge of Scrum, gain insight, and increase his competency in handling potential problems, Hakan continued to read extensively on the subject. He not only immersed himself in Scrum principles but also studied others' experiences with Scrum. He was comforted to learn that the issues faced by his team were not exclusive to them; many other teams had experienced similar issues when implementing Scrum into their working practices. He would have to work hard to help the team and manage the change that was so desperately needed. Regardless of the difficulties, he knew that Scrum was the answer, and he and the team were going to prove it!

The first sprint review event

Towards the end of the Sprint, the team's stress level escalated as they tried their utmost to fulfill the Sprint Goal. A few days before the Sprint was scheduled to end, the team asked Hakan if they could stop having the Daily Scrum and instead use the time to work on achieving the Sprint goal. He was strongly opposed to this request, as he didn't feel that they would gain much with a mere 15 extra minutes a day. Moreover, in order to reach their target, those 15 minutes would best be spent evaluating the situation as a group and reviewing strategies to decide on necessary action. The loss of transparency caused by cancelling the Daily Scrum could trigger more problems, and he wasn't keen to work outside the core Scrum framework.

In the run up to the Sprint Review event, the team continued to work tirelessly, skipping lunch breaks and making the most of every working moment. Nevertheless, it seemed unlikely that they would complete the remaining tasks before the meeting. Normally, the team would probably just fail to meet their targets and therefore not put in further effort. However, the productivity achieved through teamwork and the natural pressure of the Sprint seemed to trigger incredible short-term focus. Everyone was determined to maintain their best efforts to deliver the Sprint Goal.

With the Friday Sprint end seeming impossibly close, the team suggested that they postpone the Sprint Review until Monday morning and take the weekend to complete the necessary tasks before presenting to the stakeholders. Hakan was adamant that this was not an option. The Sprint had to be strictly adhered to, without stretching the principles. Otherwise, the slightest problem could prompt the temporary solution of extending the Sprint length, creating additional chaos and destroying the fundamental objective of maintaining sustainable productivity. As far as he was concerned, the team had to learn to be more creative under these conditions, not by extending the timescale, but by complying with the new way of working and being more organized. Rather than extending the Sprint length, which was their usual practice of gaining extra time, the team would have to change their perspective and focus on enhancing productivity and working strategies within a fixed time period. Hakan knew that the team would be resistant to this idea. Although they liked the fact that working on the Sprint meant that they didn't need to work overtime—as generally, they were working more effectively—they weren't happy when Scrum principles dictated that they must adhere to the Sprint timeframe.

The Sprint Review meeting would go ahead as planned at the end of the week, whether they were ready or not. Indeed, the team's discomfort was a sign to Hakan that Scrum was working. The more discomfort they felt, the greater the challenge to the status quo, which would hopefully stimulate change and improvement. To Hakan, it seemed like a natural stage of learning and adapting to this new way of working.

When the day of the first Sprint Review came, the team decided to keep the meeting closed, not inviting any of the stakeholders. The results were not promising, but Hakan wasn't happy with their decision. He knew that they needed to learn to face failures and successes equally, but not wanting to put more pressure on the team, he chose not to intervene.

The meeting began, and the team's general feeling of embarrassment was apparent—they looked downcast and awkward. When Johanna asked the team how the Sprint had gone, they explained that it hadn't gone exactly as planned but showed her some stories that were classified as 'Done'. Johanna was pleased to see that some things were working; though progress was minimal, her expectations had already been exceeded, since she hadn't expected much from their very first Sprint.

As they proceeded through the 'Done' Product Backlog Items, it appeared that some of them were, in fact, unfinished. A story that the team thought they had accomplished was not considered 'Done' according to the Product Owner. The team knew that they hadn't delivered all that they had forecasted, but they were surprised to see that they were in a worse situation than they had thought. According to Hakan, this was due to inadequate communication between the team and Product Owner, as well as the Product Owner's lack of active participation during the Sprint. The scope of the stories and expectations differed, highlighting the need for better communication and greater transparency in defining expectations.

They needed to encourage the Product Owner to engage with them so that they could work together as a team during the next Sprint, as the Sprint Review was not intended to be a status check or acceptance meeting for the Product Owner. Better daily collaboration to ensure that stories deemed 'Done' had actually been completed would enable them to confidently show Sprint results to their stakeholders in subsequent Review events.

The team also did not seem to have fully understood the scope of 'Done'; during the meeting, for example, they had presented Johanna with a story marked 'Done,' even though some documentation work remained outstanding. Hakan intervened, reminding them that documentation was an essential element of their 'Definition of Done' and must be included in order to fully comply with their standards. An item could only be marked 'Done' if all elements defined within the scope of 'Done' were complete. The team was even more disappointed to learn that their performance was worse than they had expected before the Review meeting. Their Velocity[20] for the first Sprint was close to zero. Despite their remarkable efforts during the Sprint, the result was a huge disappointment.

Although the team was unhappy with their results, Johanna and Hakan remained positive. For Johanna, things were better than expected, and she was confident that they could finish the project sooner than initially anticipated. She was also very impressed with the team's effort and ownership of the project, which would have a positive impact on results. Hakan was happy that the team now understood the concept of 'Done' and had learned how important it was to plan effectively at the beginning of the Sprint. These practical lessons would undoubtedly be much more permanent and powerful than any of his directives and discourse.

The first Sprint had provided a valuable opportunity for deeper understanding and improvement. The team asked for a short break before beginning the Sprint Retrospective; they had a lot to process.

---

[20] *Sprint Velocity:* Popular indication of the average amount of Product Backlog turned into an Increment of releasable product during a Sprint by a specific (composition of) a team.

The first sprint retrospective event

Hakan asked the team to relax. They would evaluate the first Sprint in the one-and-a-half-hour timebox ahead and then make decisions about what they could do at the next Sprint to increase overall performance.

They had to place the current Sprint under the spotlight, transparently identifying all the elements that had gone both well and badly in the Sprint alongside each event on the table. Afterwards, they would need to discuss which actions to take to solve the problems they had encountered. Their goal would be to come up with as many actions as possible that could help them improve and to decide which of these actions needed to be put into immediate practice in the next Sprint.

Hakan asked everyone in the room to think about what went well in the first Sprint. He stood beside the board, ready to take notes.

As the team was not at the point they had hoped to be by the end of the Sprint, they had trouble finding anything that they felt had gone well. Alex said: "We couldn't keep our promise; in fact, we couldn't even come close to it." The rest of the team agreed. Hakan needed to lead the way in freeing the team from emotional thinking in order to create the right environment in which to explicitly discuss the facts. In order to help the team focus, he needed to shake them out of their negative mindset: "We've begun to use the Scrum framework, which is a positive step. We need to focus on where we're going rather than dwelling on problems."

This advice from the Scrum Master paved the way for the team to look forward to the next Sprint. Kieran noticed the strong communication within the team. As they sat around the table, everyone was communicating animatedly with one another. They were sharing their distress, but the fact that the team was unified in confronting problems and helping each other find solutions was a positive sign.

Johanna told the team that she could see that they were taking ownership of the project and that she was very pleased with their progress. If their ownership continued at the same rate, the team would easily overcome their problems and produce the desired outcome. With contributions from all team members, they discussed several other observations about their first Sprint. The team was now able to clearly see that they had actually achieved a number of positive results during the Sprint, and this awareness gave them extra motivation.

After discussing some of the positives about their first Sprint, Hakan asked the team to look at the issues from a different angle. It was time to explore what hadn't gone well. Doing so would allow them to make further improvements and complete a clear assessment of problem areas. This time, the team was able to sort through the items more quickly. As the Sprint hadn't gone the way they had expected, it was easy to discuss their problems. Hakan noted all the items highlighted by the team on the board.

Worked Well:
- Began to experience the Scrum framework
- Strong communication within the team
- Owning problems as a team
- We supported each other

- Strong project ownership

Could Improve:
- Could not achieve our Sprint Goal
- Could not finish most of the forecasted stories
- Too many interruptions killing our focus
- Could not anticipate all the work needed to complete the stories at the Sprint Planning event
- Discovering additional tasks that we needed to work on throughout the Sprint caused stress
- Our Sprint forecast was too optimistic
- Unclear scope of stories
- Not matching our Definition of Done
- Lack of Product Owner's involvement
- No stakeholder participation in Sprint Review

While the discussion continued, Hakan couldn't help but notice that, as in the previous planning meeting, Sarah was contributing very little. Hakan encouraged her to engage by asking her specific questions, but beyond offering basic responses, she was mostly silent. When asked to participate, she gave brief summaries in line with the views of the team but did not reveal her own opinions.

Having already intervened, Hakan didn't want to push Sarah further. It was only a matter of time before she would become more actively involved. In fact, she had already shown more engagement since the Sprint Planning event, participating throughout the Sprint during their Daily Scrum and other team meetings. Hakan believed that as she felt more comfortable, the situation would resolve itself.

For their first Sprint Retrospective, the team had done fairly well. In fact, if Hakan and the timebox allowed it, they might continue discussing other problems endlessly. The main purpose of this meeting, however, was to identify clear and immediate actions for improvement. Instead of discussing problems, they needed to start thinking about specific actions that they could bring to the next Sprint.

The team acknowledged that one of the primary issues that reduced productivity and slowed down their speed was the fact that they did not clearly understand the scope of the stories at the start of the Sprint, resulting in additional tasks. Another issue was, of course, the interruptions they experienced during the Sprint.

In order to better clarify the scope of the stories, Johanna needed to express herself more clearly; otherwise, the team might continue to think that they had understood, inviting more surprises at the next Review. Johanna, however, didn't really know what to do, since she felt that she had already told the team what she wanted as best she could. According to her, the team should have asked more questions if they were uncertain about specific points. She was ready to answer their questions, but they appeared to have reached a dead end. To resolve this, Hakan decided to share an idea: his solution was to include the acceptance criteria for each story, just as they had done for the items in the setup period. These criteria would help them elaborate on and develop the needs that had to be met. In addition, the establishment of acceptance criteria might prompt more discussion between the Product Owner and the team concerning the scope of the story, leading to additional questions and, hopefully, clarification. Both Johanna and the team liked this idea. They could at least try it out in their next Sprint.

Hakan had successfully intervened, offering a helping hand at just the right time. His strong leadership seemed to increase the team's respect for him, helping to ensure that they would take his opinions and advice on board in the future.

The team continued to the next topic—the issue of their daily interruptions. When Hakan asked them to think about why they had experienced unexpected interruptions, they gave differing responses. Hakan believed that such interruptions may have been due to the fact that the team couldn't say no to the external, non-project-related demands made on them and were still trying to offer solutions as they had done previously. The team, however, disagreed—work was still coming in, and those outside the team didn't seem to respect or care about their new way of working. The additional requests were all fairly crucial; it wasn't possible to just refuse them. In fact, they pointed out, they shouldn't be expected to respond to such requests in the first place. The team was right, but Hakan knew that unless the team refused these requests, the calls from other business units would continue. In order to change this habit and direct the requests to other experts, they had to change their own habits first.

Hakan's response seemed to have convinced the team, at least somewhat. They agreed to be more careful about this in the next Sprint and would try to reassign incoming demands, though they couldn't redirect everything. Some calls were necessary and would involve working overtime in order to redirect them. They would need support from Evan and Mei in order to resolve this problem.

Hakan asked the team to think about concrete ways in which to present their concerns to their managers. Unexpectedly, Sarah had a suggestion: at the end of each Sprint, they could report external calls from outside the project, keeping a record of the amount of time they spent dealing with such calls during their Sprints. In this way, they could show how their work capacity was negatively affected due to interruptions. This approach would make it easier to convince the executives, if proven necessary.

Johanna fully supported Sarah's suggestion, since these other calls put her project at potential risk. The team considered the suggestion a positive step, although they suspected that it would not be enough to achieve the desired result. Hakan encouraged the team to give the idea a try, since he believed in both transparency and experimentation. Gathering this kind of data would also likely gain the support of Evan and Mei.

The Retrospective meeting had been successful. They had identified successes and difficulties encountered within the Sprint, as well as clear actions to implement during the next Sprint. These discussions and interactions clearly had a positive impact on the team's fusion, and Hakan was pleased to see that his team was generating ideas for improvement, indicating that they were well on their way to forming a good, cohesive team. Although they had wanted to stretch certain Scrum principles during the Sprint, the team's overall stance seemed promising, both in terms of ownership of the project and this new way of working.

Sprint 4: The Sprint Planning Event

The team hadn't managed to deliver all they had forecasted in the first three Sprints. In all three, their Velocity was much lower than anticipated. So at the last Retrospective event, they debated the idea that they had been too optimistic about size estimation. Until now, their actual effort throughout the Sprints was not reflected in the figures as their Sprint Velocity. Apparently, the problem was that size estimates were low. Therefore, the team decided to establish more realistic forecasts and to increase their size estimates at the next Planning event.

At the start of their fourth Sprint, Johanna discussed the objective and presented priority items by discussing the acceptance criteria of each story. The team didn't seem happy with what Johanna had to say, since in earlier Sprints, they had already realized the importance of understanding the Product Owner's needs. They challenged her with further questions, and after having received satisfactory answers for the first few items, they reviewed the acceptance criteria and size estimations of the now-clarified stories. As they had agreed to do at the last Retrospective meeting, they then enlarged all size estimations.

At the last Retrospective and now during the Planning event, Hakan had quietly observed the team's decision concerning size estimations. Their estimates were their own responsibility, and they were free to do with them what they wanted. In fact, the team still viewed Velocity as a kind of performance indicator, although Hakan had already explained to them that it wasn't.

Given the situation in the Planning meeting, it seemed to Hakan that the team had only increased the reference point for their relative size estimation in order to feel more successful, safe, and comfortable. Apart from the fact that the reference point had shifted from one step to another, almost nothing else had changed. The team had estimated one story as eight story points, whereas in a previous Sprint, a similar story had been assigned five story points. Similarly, they had estimated another story as 13 points, when, again, a similar item had previously been assigned eight points.

By the end of the Sprint, it seemed likely that the team's Velocity would appear to be higher, without any real improvement having taken place. However, Hakan didn't comment because although nothing had changed, the team clearly felt more relaxed. This new system, in which they had to consider time independently, was still new to them. Although Sprint Velocity was never meant to be a productivity metric, the team seemed to be placing too much emphasis on it because of old habits. However, Hakan believed that with more experience running Sprints, they would soon learn that while their estimations could help with prioritizing and planning Sprint capacities, they weren't such a big deal. Right now, there wasn't much that Hakan could do but wait. The team needed to feel comfortable, and he had to be patient. Nevertheless, if the team claimed to have achieved an increase in productivity at the next Retrospective, he would be able to reiterate the logic behind relative size estimation and Velocity.

The Planning meeting continued with Johanna discussing individual stories according to their ranking on the Backlog. Although she had initially seemed prepared, it slowly became clear that she was unable to provide answers to some of the team's important questions. She took notes, clarifying that she would get back to them on such questions, and continued to discuss other items. This unsettled the team, as they didn't want to risk pulling these stories into their Sprint without clarifying the necessary details. However, Johanna insisted that the stories were her top priority and didn't want to stray off track.

From the outset, Hakan had wanted Johanna to get more involved in the project and communicate more closely with the team, and in this case, the team was right; her lack of preparation was a problem that couldn't persist. The team had every right for the final decision concerning Sprint items to be pulled into the Sprint. On the other hand, the team's resistance to Johanna's order of priority could cause tension between them.

For now, Hakan asked both sides to offer a temporary solution, postponing discussion of the matter until the upcoming Retrospective. Although Johanna refused to back down, she did offer a suggestion: she would not change the order of priority for items that were still unclear, as they needed to be delivered as soon as possible. However, she would respond to their outstanding questions immediately after the meeting. The team could now make magnitude estimates for items currently under discussion and select those that they would pull into the Sprint. If, depending on Johanna's answers to their questions, the situation changed, and the pulled items conflicted with their current expectations, they would be able to discuss them together and make relevant changes to the Sprint scope.

The team cautiously considered Johanna's suggestion. They weren't keen on pulling an item and then having to discuss changes, but they were aware of her good intentions, so they accepted her proposal. They agreed that they could change the Sprint scope later, if necessary. It had already been more than two hours since they began the Planning event, and their unanswered questions and ensuing discussions had taken a lot of time, leaving them little space to work on creating their tasks and related Sprint strategy. They needed to quickly decide on the Sprint scope and move on.

With concerns about previous Sprints and the fear of failing to fulfill their forecasts, the team was careful to pull fewer stories this time. Johanna felt that the team was working diligently, but Hakan wanted to push them a bit further. He felt that they could accomplish more in the time they had, but the team was resistant. They certainly didn't want to promise more than they could achieve. However, they agreed that if things went better than anticipated, they would let Johanna know and take on more work accordingly. Despite Hakan's wishes, the team was determined not to change the scope.

After a short break, and with almost an hour before the end of the timebox, the team began to identify all story-related tasks. They had made definitive progress, identifying realistic tasks and forecasting them without as much debate as in previous Sprints.

Hakan recalled that during the first Sprint, the team had added almost as many new tasks as had been defined at the Planning meeting. Now, they seemed better equipped to decide on most of the tasks at the Planning meeting, as they were gaining a clearer understanding of the project and were used to working together. Such improvement would undoubtedly prove beneficial for the team, enabling them to formulate and implement good Sprint strategy.

Are daily scrums really necessary?

On their fourth Sprint, the team was determined to deliver their goal. This time, they wanted to be able to attend the Review event with confidence. Their motivation was evident, so much so that they arrived to work early in the morning, focused on completing the tasks left over from the day before. They went out for a quick lunch together and immediately got back to work. Everyone was aware of their responsibilities and were doing their best to fulfill them.

As he gained more competency with Scrum, Hakan continued to actively monitor the team. As they had continued to progress over the last few weeks, they had also been running into more impediments. Their list of issues was growing, with problems in test environments and latency in user acceptance tests both negatively impacting their efficiency. Hakan spent a lot of time trying to deal with these impediments while keeping up the team's motivation. He also met frequently with Johanna to assist her and encourage her active engagement in the process, as he didn't want to run the risk of losing her to outside tasks.

Problems began to emerge regarding the starting hours and effectiveness of the Daily Scrum. Initially, Hakan hadn't interfered, even though the meetings were beginning a little later than they should. He didn't want to be perceived as a normative despot intent on making the team's lives more difficult, but increasingly, the team was arriving late and not using meeting times effectively.

The Sprint was days from completion, and the team arrived to the office at their usual time and began to work on their tasks.

However, Hakan didn't see anyone championing the Daily Scrum, even though it should already have begun. He had to intervene.

After prompted by Hakan, the team gathered in front of the Scrum Board, but within minutes, they were ready to return to their desks. Hakan said that he wanted to take a few minutes with them to talk about the Daily Scrum. He had observed that for a few days now, their Daily Scrum meetings had been delayed, and even today, he had to remind them to start—why? What had happened, and why weren't they taking the meetings seriously? Michael questioned whether they really needed the Daily Scrum; they were working under strict time constraints, and they wanted the Sprint to succeed. He pointed out that they were together all day, continually discussing the issues they needed to address, and he didn't see the value in spending 10-15 minutes each morning on this meeting.

Hakan was prepared to respond to Michael's reaction. He had observed the team over the past few days and had seen that they were highly focused on their individual tasks; he also realized that they didn't spend enough time together discussing how best to achieve the Sprint Goal. One example of their lack of communication was highlighted by a situation involving Michael and Alex, who discussed and instigated a change concerning one of the solutions to an item but failed to inform Sarah of the change. It took Hakan flagging this for Michael and Alex to realize that this had been the case. Their failure to discuss the changes with Sarah meant that she would have to make adjustments to the test case scenarios that she had already written and implemented. She, too, was hearing about these updates for the first time, thanks to Hakan's observations. Without these updates, her test cases would be irrelevant. She had to be kept up to date, or the result would be excessive work and lost time.

This was a small example of simple miscommunication, occurring despite the fact that the team worked around the same desks all day and were in constant contact. The Daily Scrum was meant to prevent disruption to the flow of information, to facilitate necessary actions in achieving the Sprint Goal, and to strengthen team spirit. Hakan's observations proved that the team had been misguided in objecting to the Daily Scrum. He stressed the importance of holding regular, punctual meetings—to ensure effectiveness, the team must recognize the value in complying with this vital element of the Scrum framework.

As a deterrent for lateness, Sarah suggested imposing a fine for late arrivals at meetings, with the fine rising incrementally for each minute late. No one objected to this, but having read that fines weren't a useful deterrent, Hakan wasn't convinced of its value. For him, it was enough to see that the team cared enough to change their habits. Still, the team seemed enthusiastic about trying Sarah's idea, and although Hakan was concerned, he was pleased by their new attitude. Sarah's proposal would be actioned as an experiment, and if it didn't have the desired result, they could bring the issue back to the agenda.

Team spirit

The team proudly entered the Retrospective event of their fourth Sprint. For the first time, they had fulfilled the Sprint Goal and had even delivered more than forecasted in their initial plan. The Development Team, Scrum Master, and Product Owner were extremely satisfied with the outcome.

The team was keen to discuss improvements, and all agreed that they had achieved their targets in completing their Sprint Goal. Sprint Velocity had clearly increased. Hakan asked the team to identify and discuss possible reasons for their increased delivery.

The team believed that Sprint Velocity had increased because they had a good plan from the very beginning of the Sprint. Of course, there had been some mishaps and surprises that required them to make changes to their initial plans, but fortunately, the team had noticed them early on and had responded immediately.

"So," said Hakan, "As a team, we have created a successful team game with good communication by keeping transparency high throughout the Sprint. Actually, it seems that we have really started to feel like the A-Team." He wrote items on the board: good communication, successful team play, good planning, high transparency... But what were the factors involved in these successes? He wanted the team to examine and discuss them in more detail.

The team thought that time was the underlying reason for better communication; for over two months, they had been working together around the same table, going out to lunch, bonding, and overcoming problems. Over time, they had become used to each other. Everyone had come to understand the others' moods, responses, and work habits. Hakan added that he saw significant improvement in the team's relationships and that friendships had clearly been formed. Now, unlike at the beginning, it wasn't just different people sitting around the same table, trying to find solutions. They had become cohesive, working in harmony to reach their shared goals. The A-Team was a success!

Hakan was pleased with the formation of team spirit, which was even now readily observable. They seemed to be able to speak freely on any topic, discuss it amongst themselves, and reach a satisfactory conclusion. The development of friendships and camaraderie within the team meant that a problem for any individual team member was a problem for the whole team. The team's mutual support of one another meant that these problems were quickly resolved, and, in turn, this recently-attained team spirit and solidarity was positively reflected in their productivity.

However, Hakan was also aware that becoming a team was not a straightforward process. Though the team had reached an equilibrium and had begun to demonstrate it with good performance, the process of change would continue. Challenging project objectives were still ahead of them, and with new obstacles, team spirit could still be negatively affected. Hakan would continue to closely observe the team, prepared to support them in the face of potential stumbling blocks.

Undoubtedly, team spirit was an important factor that enabled the team to plan and deliver results. However, the questions asked to the Product Owner, as well as the acceptance criteria created collectively as a team, also played a significant role in clarifying the team's objectives. Because they were getting used to the project, they were now able to better determine where they might face difficulties in implementing requests and were therefore better prepared to make and adjust plans accordingly. Because of this, they didn't encounter many critical surprises that would reduce their effectiveness in the Sprint. The factors they discussed—including good understanding of the scope, effective planning, increased transparency with Scrum, and team spirit and motivation—were also reflected in their increased Sprint Velocity. At this point, Hakan reiterated that velocity was not an indicator of productivity. He also explained that the increase in Velocity was partially due to the increase in size estimates established at the start of the Sprint. In fact, the team had shifted and increased their reference point so that the Velocity increased, too.

Now they could begin to discuss problematic areas that could be improved. Before this, though, Johanna wanted to add that the team had achieved more than they had forecasted at the start of the Sprint. This was an unexpected but very positive result for her, and she was pleased with the team's performance. In addition, the team, having realized that the target they had established in the Sprint would be complete before the end of the scheduled Sprint time, and immediately contacted her about pulling in new items to work on. The fact that Johanna recognized the team's effort and commitment and was pleased with their accomplishments made Hakan and the team very happy. They were pleased to see that their efforts were appreciated.

It was obvious that the team felt more comfortable with this

Sprint, so they had difficulty finding any improvement areas to discuss. Hakan asked them to reflect on the issues they had encountered in the last Sprint Planning event, when they had struggled with some of the items that weren't entirely clear. In order to prevent this from recurring in upcoming Sprints, they should discuss potential problems and try to come up with solutions now.

The team knew that Hakan was right but felt that the unclear scope had largely been due to Johanna. In order to prepare for the Planning Meeting, they thought, she had to work harder to clarify the stories. In response, Johanna replied that it was impossible for her to anticipate questions that might arise because the stories involved technical matters that she didn't have knowledge of; this was why she needed the team's help. Kieran replied, "Then Johanna and Michael can work together on the stories that might be the subject of the next Sprint during the actual Sprint." This suggestion sounded reasonable to everyone, including Michael and Johanna. Hakan, though, suggested that they hold a team Product Backlog Refinement[21] activity during the Sprint. He believed that instead of involving just Johanna and Michael, there was more benefit in strengthening communication and teamwork as a group. Otherwise, Michael would be functioning as a go-between for the group, which was unnecessary and potentially risky. Though Michael was a competent analyst, there could be problems that he wouldn't be able to identify on his own.

Kieran and Alex didn't seem pleased with Hakan's proposal, as they'd already spent a significant amount of time in meetings. The team was not happy about losing more time in a Refinement activity. Because Sarah also shared their concerns, Hakan

---

[21] *Product Backlog Refinement: The recurring activity in a Sprint through which the Product Owner and the Development Team add granularity to future Product Backlog.*

realized that he would need to outline the details and benefits of Backlog Refinement. It certainly wasn't a waste of time, he said, as it would increase the team's effectiveness and further clarify upcoming stories. It would also help to consolidate team spirit and trigger creativity. The purpose of the meeting was not to analyze—analysis activities were already being held with the help and guidance of Michael, who communicated with Johanna when necessary. The aim of this meeting would be to help identify the steps that Johanna would need to take in order to clarify stories, involving a sharing of ideas that would be enriched by the team's input. As a result of this collaboration, the team would be more actively involved in the project's vision. Moreover, the meeting could help them produce some creative solutions, allowing them to see the bigger picture and ensuring that Johanna and the entire team were prepared for upcoming Sprints. This would make Planning events more efficient than they had been in the past. Contrary to their beliefs, the activity which initially seemed to be a waste of time would in fact help them to see their way ahead and increase productivity.

Although they seemed unconvinced, the team couldn't really dispute Hakan's stance on this matter. They respected him and knew from previous experience that listening to his suggestions would benefit them. They agreed to try the Refinement activity over the course of the next few Sprints, and if it didn't work out, they could then consider discontinuing it. He asked them when they would like to schedule it. Johanna wanted to hold the activity immediately after the Sprint Planning, if possible. However, holding two meetings in a row would be challenging, requiring the team to switch focus from thinking about the actual Sprint Goal to the overall picture. Hakan asked them to consider another proposal.

After some discussion, the team decided to hold the Refinement activity on their first Friday afternoon of the Sprint, two hours before the end of work. Since Friday afternoons weren't very productive times, the meeting might give them the motivation they needed. Everyone accepted this proposal.

Before finishing the meeting, Hakan also asked the team to discuss the interruptions they had experienced during the Sprint. They had recorded rough data on the amount of time they had spent dealing with interruptions over the last three Sprints. It showed that these interruptions were steadily decreasing. The people to whom they had already transferred tasks could now move forward on their own without much need for further assistance, so it appeared that the issue had essentially been resolved.

Still, Michael continued to be interrupted more than any of the other team members. Although these interruptions didn't affect the team's ability to keep up their Sprint pace, they could potentially create problems in the future. Hakan believed that if Michael could invest more of his time in the Scrum project, the team's overall productivity would increase. Michael had a background in software development, which, in addition to helping with analysis, could also help the team during bottlenecks. Michael pointed out that he was already doing as much as he could, his teammates nodding in affirmation. He tried to explain the reason behind the interruptions: "This project is of course my first priority, but as I told you recently, Hakan, I don't want to break away from my own department too much, as I would lose touch with what's going on there. When this project ends, I'll be going back to my old department again, and I don't want my return process to be too difficult. So I don't mind the occasional inconvenience of having to deal with other projects together with this one. It helps to motivate me."

Hakan had initially thought that David would be the main obstacle affecting Michael's focus on the project, so he'd kept a close eye on it. Now, he was surprised to find that the reason for Michael's continued interruptions was not due to his manager but to Michael, himself. But Hakan could see Michael's point. It was true that this was the first time that the company had used Scrum, and nobody knew what to expect once the project was over. This uncertainty was bound to affect Michael—it was perfectly understandable that he didn't want to damage his affiliation with his own department. His problem didn't seem to be with Scrum but with insecurity about the future. Because Hakan didn't want to demotivate or even lose him, he decided not to press the matter any further.

Michael's multiple responsibilities weren't currently an issue for the rest of the team—they were happy with his involvement and enjoyed working with him. Therefore, Hakan didn't want to push them and risk affecting their motivation. "Well then," he said, "I understand your situation, Michael, and of course you are free to do whatever you want, as long as it doesn't negatively affect this project. We can still keep collecting data on our interruptions, even though the problem seems to be resolved." Even though the team didn't consider Michael's situation a problem, they were happy to continue monitoring and maintaining the relevant data. Hakan asked if Michael had anything more to add, or if the team had anything further to raise regarding the Sprint's progress. Since no one had any further input, Hakan finished by reminding them about the Refinement meeting.

Improving communication with the product owner

The fifth Sprint was progressing as planned. If there were no surprises, the team would be able to achieve the Sprint Goal, as they had previously. This time, however, they were under additional pressure, as the next Sprint Review event would be attended by a significant number of stakeholders. Therefore, it was vital for them to seamlessly achieve the Sprint Goal in order to host a successful Review meeting.

As planned, the team had a Refinement meeting scheduled for the first Friday afternoon of the Sprint. However, during their Daily Scrum, Hakan realized that the team seemed preoccupied with continuing the Sprint in preparation for the forthcoming Sprint Review and weren't really willing to spend their time on Backlog Refinement. Aware of the team's escalating stress levels, he gave a short pep talk at the end of the morning meeting, assuring them of his confidence in their ability to meet their targets, as they were already making excellent progress. Hakan's priority was that the team should feel relaxed but motivated, as further stress would negatively impact their performance in the coming week. With this in mind, he asked the team to keep the afternoon's Refinement Meeting on the schedule so that they would be able to manage their upcoming backlog items as a group. Working together, they could try to keep the meeting as brief as possible in order to reduce time pressure.

When they met for the Refinement meeting, Hakan began by introducing the purpose and format of the meeting. Johanna was keen to know how the current Sprint was going, and some team members also had queries for Johanna about the current

Sprint's items, though such issues weren't on the agenda of the Refinement meeting. Nevertheless, Hakan didn't object to providing some time for Johanna and the team to share their thoughts. After all, good communication between the team and Product Owner was essential for the smooth running of the project.

After they had discussed the issues of the current Sprint, Johanna began to review the Backlog and shared upcoming top-priority stories with the team. There had been few changes to the Product Backlog since the previous Planning event, and it was soon clear to everyone that some of the items should be broken down into smaller parts and dealt with separately. The team also proposed several alternative solutions for Johanna's new requests. Handling these new stories in line with their recommendations would allow the stories to be implemented more quickly and easily. Johanna was excited about many of their suggestions and revised the backlog accordingly. But she wasn't able to make a decision on all of their proposals, as some would have to be discussed with other stakeholders. After these discussions, a decision could be made according to the stakeholders' feedback. The meeting seemed to have prompted an efficient exchange of ideas. Johanna noted down some of the team's concerns and questions; with the remainder of the Sprint time, she would be able to work through these issues and provide the team with clearer answers at the next Sprint Planning event.

The meeting ended early, and Hakan was curious to hear everyone's comments and thoughts. He asked the group to briefly evaluate how the meeting had gone. Overall, they seemed satisfied, as they now better understood the stories and had fulfilled some of the requirements with solutions that would make their worklife easier. Their discussions had enabled Johanna, too, to ask a few more pertinent questions on some important points she hadn't previously considered, and she now had notes to discuss with the stakeholders. Their overall conclusion was that the meeting had been very constructive and was an important forum for information exchange between the team and the Product Owner. In order to enhance collaboration, they decided to continue to invest in this activity.

Feedback Time

The Review event was held in a larger meeting room (rather than the team room) to allow for the increased number of attendees. The team arrived first, confident and proud at having fulfilled the Sprint Goal. Johanna and the other stakeholders gradually filtered in. Hakan and Evan arrived together—they were the driving force behind introducing Scrum to the company, and this meeting was especially important for them, as success would encourage further uptake of Scrum on other projects. Stakeholder support was essential in achieving their long-term goals.

Johanna thanked everyone for coming to the event. She began by introducing the members of the A-Team, continuing with an outline of the project, overall project objectives, and the goal of the Sprint. She then called on Hakan to briefly run through the Scrum framework and their new way of working. Afterwards, the team began to share the actual increment of the software. Moving on to their current situation, Johanna expressed her satisfaction with the Development Team's outstanding performance on the project. The team had done a great job—they had achieved the Sprint Goal and had brought the product to a minimum usable point. These successes, as well as Johanna's praise for the team's achievements, were evidence enough for the stakeholders; they were clearly pleased with what they were hearing. While the team continued to outline the working functionalities, which the stakeholders weren't accustomed to seeing in such a short period of time, the participants began to ask additional questions to better understand the usage and give feedback on improvement areas. Johanna and the team gave clear, comprehensive answers to the stakeholder's questions.

Their responses showed total commitment to the project—they had evidently taken full ownership, further impressing the stakeholders. Johanna took notes of the stakeholders' comments, which would potentially be added to the Product Backlog as new items. Stakeholder participation would enable her to detect and define further improvements to the product.

After the team had finished answering questions on the increment, Johanna prepared to review the next steps and the state of the Product Backlog, but before she began, Kristen asked how they could use the existing functionalities that had been produced. Johanna seemed confused by this question. Kristen clarified, addressing the other stakeholders: "We would like to start using the current version of the software. Many of the features that have been developed could be used in our work and would add value to our daily lives. I could start using some of the reports that you have shown us. I currently spend a lot of time gathering the information you just presented to us and mostly need to call IT for additional support. But if I can search the data myself using this new system you've demonstrated, it will be easier. I'm not sure if anyone else agrees with me."

Hakan, Evan, and the team were pleased that Kristen wanted to start using the software straight away. Michael took the lead and offered to define user accounts for those that wanted to get started. This was excellent news for the stakeholders; it seemed that everyone in the room was eager to use the new system as soon as possible.

Johanna and the team agreed to give the stakeholders access to the system by creating the necessary user credentials. This was real progress, and the stakeholders were delighted with this unexpected opportunity. Customarily, they would have had to wait until the project had been underway for eight to nine months before they would see any benefit, and this was just the third month. This was undeniable proof of the benefits of Scrum, and the business units felt that they were being well-rewarded.

Kristen and the other stakeholders thanked the team and asked Hakan if it would be possible for these Sprint Review events to happen more regularly, and if stakeholders could be kept informed with updates. Hakan was so happy with the outcome of the meeting that he didn't hesitate to accept, confirming that stakeholders would be welcome to attend the bi-weekly Sprint Review events. It had been an extraordinarily successful meeting that had exceeded every expectation.

Evolving Transformation Action List

The A-Team was increasing the momentum it had achieved in the last few Sprints. While the seventh Sprint of the project had yet to be completed, they had achieved significant progress, and their motivation was accelerating. Everything was going well for the team and the project, and Hakan no longer had to remind them of Scrum principles— they had gained the basic Scrum reflex. The meetings began on time, the Timebox was complied with, and the Product Backlog and Scrum Board were maintained. Of course, this didn't mean that they were a perfect team and no longer needed their Scrum Master. On the contrary, Hakan knew that he needed to work harder to maintain the effectiveness of these newly-acquired habits.

Hakan remembered the Transformation Action List that he had created long before he started the project. He was so engrossed in the team's day-to-day work that he hadn't had time to revisit the plan in a long while. Now seemed like a good time to evaluate the current situation and revise the plan accordingly.

While revising the Transformation Action List and reflecting on the overall process during the previous four months, Hakan realized that he had mainly focused on helping consolidate the team to achieve immediate success by coaching them within the Scrum framework. This had delivered the desired results, and they were now well-established in working together as a Scrum Team. Scrum had enabled them to realize their own strengths and manifested mutual trust. From the fifth Sprint, they had begun to produce outcomes that garnered praise and delighted the business unit. Although Hakan was satisfied with the team's positive mood and their ownership of Scrum, he believed that there were still many points to improve upon. Firstly, he felt that the team would benefit from adopting 'Kaizen' culture, which would help the team identify potential areas for self-improvement and work on them independently, without Hakan's direct guidance. There was still a long way to go before the team would be able to achieve this, however, having only recently adapted to the new way of working with Scrum. It was a process that would require them to adopt a deeper perspective on continuous improvement, but he knew that a gradual, planned approach to introducing elements of Kaizen culture would spark the team's interest.

Retrospective Events were extremely important to the formation of a Scrum Team's Kaizen culture, and Hakan questioned whether the A-Team was getting as much out of these meetings as they could be. In recent successful Sprints, the outputs from the Retrospective Events hadn't been satisfactory; because things were going well enough, the team seemed a bit too comfortable, causing them to become complacent about identifying areas for improvement. Waiting for things to go wrong before making improvements went against Scrum principles. In order to avoid falling into old patterns or a 'good enough' mentality, they needed to understand and assimilate a perspective of continuous improvement as a fundamental part of their daily lives. Only then would they become a high-performing, productive, and fully self-organized team.

Addressing this issue became Hakan's priority. He would speak with the team at the next Retrospective, pointing out that they hadn't been using these events effectively enough and should therefore try different strategies to maximize their value. He had already raised this issue several times before, but even though the team seemed to approve of Hakan, none of them had volunteered to take any action to resolve it. No matter what method they tried for Retrospectives, lasting results would be elusive as long as the team felt there was no need to improve. Hakan would have to try an alternative approach to help them understand the importance of these events and to ignite the first spark of Kaizen culture in the team's mindset.

Hakan thought that he needed to surprise the team by approaching the issue from an unexpected angle so that he could help them see that there was always potential for improvement, even in matters in which they appeared to be succeeding. Constantly striving for progress and refinement of practices was essential to the spirit of Scrum.

His first consideration concerned the Scrum fundamentals. He began to evaluate previous events of the Scrum framework. The Planning Events were now functioning adequately, though in the early days, the team had essentially muddled along, sometimes without the necessary clarity on how they should be proceeding. Fortunately, the Refinement activities had helped to provide this clarity.

In assessing the Daily Scrums, Hakan realized that they could play a vital role in improving the team's perspective. The meetings began punctually, fit the Timebox, and generally considered the three main questions, but the team lacked motivation in these events. They had become habitual, and consequently, they were not getting the most out of their meetings; they lacked the necessary transparency, communication, focus, and consolidation of team spirit. They did not see the value in these morning events and were not contributing as they should, so informal scattered discussions happened throughout the day as they tried to establish how best to achieve their goals. If they used the Daily Scrum effectively, they could progress more synchronously towards their Sprint Goal without frequent interruptions during the day. Hakan decided to raise this issue at the next Retrospective, where he would suggest that the team review their approach to the Daily Scrum.

Hakan reviewed the past four-month period based on the progress of the A-Team and added a number of new items to the Transformation Action List. He also considered his own role as a change agent and how best to support the spread of change. Things were going well on the CRM project, and team morale was high. It was time to focus on his plans for the expansion of Scrum within the company.

Hakan reviewed his previous actions to maintain momentum within the group. At the beginning of the CRM project, he had informed business unit managers about Scrum and the forthcoming process of change. These small, informative meetings had proven useful, reflected in the fact that the team had not been disrupted by sudden changes during their Sprints, and that the obstacles they faced had been quickly resolved with the support of the business unit.

In addition, the participation of Kristen and the other stakeholders in the Review Events since the fifth Sprint had been highly beneficial in raising the profile of Scrum, as well as awareness of the team's achievements within the business unit. Hakan believed that successful completion of the CRM project would convince Kristen and the other units to consider other new projects that may benefit from Scrum. Although the project was not yet completed, he could provide Kristen and her team with a simple survey to assess their experience of the Scrum process thus far; positive results could then be shared with other business units to encourage their future participation. As Kristen was notoriously hard to please, her positive support of Scrum would be difficult to dismiss.

Now was the time to introduce Scrum to a wider audience outside the CRM project and provide clear, in-depth information about it. Building on current awareness triggered by the first pilot team, Hakan could encourage the A-Team to discuss their experiences up to this point. It would be much more persuasive for people to hear about Scrum firsthand, from their peers who had directly experienced it.

Hakan now had a clear plan for his Transformation Action List. With his goal of spreading the news about Scrum, he devised a long to-do list, together with some new items for the A-Team.

TRANSFORMATION ACTION LIST

TARGET	ACTION
Start pilot project	Scrum Training for the team
	Team kickoff and handling preparations
	Start the first Sprint
Attract attention and create interest in change	Inform the management and stakeholders about Scrum and its new way of working
	Involve stakeholders in the process and keep them updated
	Continue stakeholder involvement in the Sprint Reviews
Establish Scrum Reflex	Getting the team used to working within the Scrum framework
	Form team norms
	Enhance transparency
	Enhance teamwork
	Support self-organization behavior
Trigger Kaizen Culture	Enhance effectiveness of Daily Scrums
	Improve Retrospective Events
	Invest in capability building of team members
Scaling the Transformation	Distribute a business survey and collect stakeholder insights about the pilot project
	Organize A-Team experience-sharing events about new way of working
	Look for new pilot projects

Sprint 7: The Sprint Retrospective

The team was now thoroughly used to working with Scrum. At the Retrospective Meeting of their seventh Sprint, they seemed cheerful and relaxed, proud of having achieved their Sprint Goal. Everything was going well, and the Review had been positive, so they didn't believe they had much to worry about at the Retrospective. Chatting casually with their teammates, they felt that they could now comfortably wait for the Sprint and the day to end.

As usual, Hakan allowed the team to conduct the meeting without interference on his part. But from his perspective, it appeared that the team was treating the Retrospective Event as an opportunity for self-congratulation; little was offered in the name of improvement. Having waited for the team to celebrate their achievements, he couldn't help but interrupt: "Hey guys, I agree with you. We had a good Sprint. We met our goal. Customers are really satisfied. I'm happy too, but…" Without allowing him to finish, Michael interjected: "Yet another 'but' from Hakan! Hakan, to be honest, we are all pleased, and everyone else is, too, but for some reason, we can't please you." Everyone laughed, and Hakan realized that he should explain himself: "Unfortunately, Michael, this is one of the challenges of being a Scrum Master. You can never be complacent. You must force yourself and the team to do more and more. Of course I'm really happy with what we've achieved; however, I think there are a lot of ways we can improve. Because I know you all have great potential. Like in Retrospective Meetings, we always struggle to identify actions for improvement. It's true, things are going well, but that doesn't mean that everything is perfect and that it can't get any better." The team knew very well what he meant and had to agree that there was always room for even greater achievement.

Because it was the end of the week, and they couldn't help but feel like they deserved to relax and celebrate their success, it was difficult for the team to focus on ways to improve themselves and their performance. Hakan talked about Kaizen and the importance of the Retrospective for enhancing their progress. It was an opportunity to make observations and analyses of the Sprint, and of the way they work.

Sarah asked Hakan what kind of improvements he had in mind. She felt that the main problem with Retrospective Events was not that the team didn't care but that they struggled to find things to improve upon. Everything was going well, and at least for the short term, there didn't seem to be anything they needed to work on further. Sarah sounded sincere, and her perspective seemed to be representative of the team's, so Hakan asked her to think about the atmosphere of the Daily Scrums. The team was surprised— there was no downtime in the Daily Scrum. It was just a short and simple meeting, and there didn't seem to be any room for improvement concerning the atmosphere, they thought. He reminded them about the purpose of the Daily Scrum. They were clearly abiding by the rules of the meeting, but were they using it to its optimum? Were they using it to focus on the Sprint Goal and to synchronize as a team, boosting team morale and increasing productivity? Or had it just become a habitual, daily routine with little appreciated value?

The team considered Hakan's questions. It was true that the Daily Scrums weren't much fun and seemed a bit pointless, and they could happily have discontinued them. He was right that they should use them as an opportunity to share more, and maybe they could use the time more effectively. But they couldn't really see what more they could do. Every day at the same time, and in the same place, they gathered as a team and responded to all three questions. Hakan suggested that they try looking at it from the Kaizen perspective. If they examined the process carefully and discussed it in detail, they would surely find a better approach.

"So, what are you proposing, Hakan?" asked Kieran, who couldn't help but wonder what Hakan could see that the team couldn't. In response, Hakan suggested that they prepare a list of items about running a successful Daily Scrum. Throughout the next Sprint, they could reflect on this list and then, at the next Retrospective, use it to self-evaluate their Daily Scrums. Of course, he may be wrong. Maybe they wouldn't be able to change things, but at least it was worth trying. It may even spark a bit of Kaizen culture within the team. They agreed to Hakan's proposal— it wouldn't be too arduous, and making the Daily Scrum more enjoyable and motivational would be a bonus.

SPRINT 9: THE SPRINT REVIEW

As usual, the Review Event was packed. Since the fifth Sprint, all of the stakeholders continued to attend, showing their level of interest in the project and their satisfaction with the progress being made. The Review meetings were fun and fostered a positive atmosphere in which creative ideas and suggestions were shared.

This time, the team had achieved more on the Sprint than they had forecasted. One reason for this was the work they had done to improve Daily Scrums in recent Sprints. With the increasing effectiveness of the Daily Scrum, the team had learned to start the day in a more energetic, well-planned manner. Their increased energy and in-team information sharing had helped to increase productivity, reflected in the positive result of the team's Sprint.

The stakeholders were extremely satisfied with the team's delivered results and the status they had achieved. Over the last month, the stakeholders had used the system intensively. Kristen thanked the team for their work and had a suggestion regarding the rest of the project. "We've come a long way on the project. We've started using the system and can see real benefits in our daily work. As far as I'm concerned, we don't need to continue the project to complete all of the remaining requests. There are one or two missing elements that are important to us that need to be finished. Then we can end the project much earlier than the targeted time. The remaining requirements aren't too critical, as we don't need them at the moment. But since we're already using the system, I anticipate that further needs will arise in the future. These can all be dealt with later, on a second project for this system, but I think we're nearly ready to bring the project to a close and move the team to other important projects." Johanna and the other stakeholders agreed. Apart from a few functionalities and improvements, nothing critical had been omitted. Everyone agreed that they first needed to identify which elements needed to be finished and which could be left for the future. Then the project could be considered complete. With the matter settled, Kristen began to share her opinion about the items that needed to be addressed as top priority.

Hakan followed these discussions closely and excitedly. Thanks to the team and the Scrum, the real needs of the product were already being met faster than usual. In fact, due to the team's high performance and the removal of unnecessary requests from the project scope, the project seemed to be finished a few months earlier than predicted. This was a great achievement for scaling this new way of working within the company.

Kristen and the stakeholders continued the discussion about the Product Backlog, but as they were close to the end of their allocated time and were drifting away from the focus of the Review Event, Hakan intervened: "Kristen, your proposal is excellent, and we definitely need to check the Product Backlog together. But as this is not the subject of the Review meeting and we don't have much time left, let's do it next week at a more suitable time." The team agreed with Hakan—as the Product Owner, Johanna could have this discussion with the stakeholders at a later time, and together, they could identify which stories still needed to be implemented and which were unnecessary.

At the end of the meeting, Kristen and Evan stayed back to speak with Hakan. When Kristen thanked him for his efforts and achievements, Hakan was quick to point out that their success was due to the hard work of the team and their use of Scrum. The confidence that he had placed in Scrum from the very start seemed justified; delivering high-quality products and reducing the time frame was a fantastic outcome for the team and the stakeholders, and he knew that there was still more to achieve with Scrum. The support of Kristen and other managers was pivotal in his plan to spread the use of Scrum throughout the company, and this was his opportunity to broach it with them: "The project is going well, as you said, and certainly the results of Scrum are obvious. As you know, we have recently conducted a simple survey which shows that both the team and the stakeholders are very satisfied with this new way of working. Maybe we could get together to discuss how we can transfer the success of this project to our other projects so that the whole company can benefit."

Kristen and Evan didn't need any more convincing—Evan had been behind the project from the start, and resolving difficulties faced by the team was important for everyone. "I absolutely agree with you, Hakan," said Evan, "Kristen and Mei's support is very important to us. If it's okay with them, as IT, I would like to meet up to further discuss new potential projects for Scrum."

It seemed they were all in agreement, and having checked their calendars for the following week, a meeting was scheduled.

Taking Action to Spread Change

Hakan's review meeting with Kristen, Evan, and Mei was going well, and as shown by the survey, Kristen and her team were satisfied with the progress of the CRM project. They could see the potential in applying Scrum to some of the other projects they managed. Kristen's priority, as always, was that their projects could be completed quickly and efficiently by the IT department, and she didn't want to interfere with the Project Management Office or the IT department in deciding which practice they used, Scrum or otherwise. She confirmed that she and her team would support them in achieving whatever shared goal they chose. Understandably, she didn't want to take responsibility for future problems by directing them on an issue outside her field of expertise. She clarified that she would support the implementation of Scrum, but the decision was ultimately the responsibility of the Project Management Office and IT department.

Speaking on behalf of the IT department, Evan observed that working with Scrum had not only increased productivity and quality but had also significantly increased the team's motivation. Members of the A-Team reported higher levels of work satisfaction which, in turn, had positively impacted the speed and quality of their work. Evan had always believed that Scrum was the right choice for the company and felt that it should be broadly implemented as quickly as possible. It was important to prepare the rest of the department for Scrum's implementation, and they were ready for it. Other teams within the IT department were also interested in Scrum and were keen to be involved in one of its projects. Only one or two managers within the department were less enthusiastic, but Evan had no doubt that he could convince them.

As Head of the PMO, Mei was impressed by the results of the CRM project and the satisfaction of the business unit and IT department. News of their success had been spreading throughout the company, and she was interested in the viability of applying Scrum to more projects. However, Mei seemed a bit more cautious than Evan and Hakan. She could see that the work on the pilot project had exceeded expectations, but it was still not complete. In her opinion, the project's success could have been due to chance, and Scrum may not work in the same way on other projects. She had seen the impressive levels of commitment and dedication that the A-Team had shown, but achieving the same degree of ownership and self-sacrifice may not be possible with everyone. It was impossible to predict whether Scrum would be successful without this sense of ownership, which Mei believed to be the primary factor in the CRM project's success. She had already discussed these concerns with Hakan prior to the meeting.

Hakan maintained that ownership and commitment were features of the Scrum framework, itself. With a self-organizing team at its center, Scrum was designed to empower individuals. Team members had gained confidence and become more productive because of the freedom that this self-organization gave them. But Mei still seemed unconvinced. She conceded that almost everyone in the IT department was keen to implement Scrum, but this may just be because it was a new trend. In her opinion, they may not all be able to maintain the same enthusiasm and achieve the same successes by adopting Scrum.

The meeting concluded with all factors having been considered and all parties agreeing to continue introducing Scrum on a few new projects, while remaining cautious yet open to the benefits of Scrum. In this manner, they could continue to observe Scrum and monitor its returns on a larger scale before reevaluating its role in future plans.

Hakan asked Mei and Evan to join him in evaluating which forthcoming projects to select as the next Scrum candidates, and Kristen promised to ask her team if they had any potential projects that would be suitable for upcoming pilots. Hakan planned to encourage active participation from all parties in the process, using every opportunity to invest in growing collaboration within the company.

Overall, Hakan was pleased with the outcome, though he still wanted to make more extreme decisions for radical change as soon as possible. He believed in Scrum wholeheartedly; the positive atmosphere that it had brought to the company proved that Scrum's success would snowball and that the radical change that he hoped for was indeed attainable.

Chapter III:
The Wind of Change

Selecting additional projects

The new pilot projects were pivotal to fundamentally changing working practice within the company. Achieving significant successes in these new projects would prove that Scrum's success on the CRM project was not due to mere chance, thereby increasing Scrum's impetus, strengthening the wind of change, and enabling the benefits of Scrum to spread throughout the company. With this in mind, Hakan began to examine potential projects before meeting with the others to discuss them. He reviewed all possible projects with similar criteria, as he had when selecting the first pilot project. This time, however, he added a few new criteria.

One of these new criteria was that the projects selected should belong to different business units so as to access a broader spectrum of applications, experiences, and achievements. Achieving success across a diverse range of projects would strengthen the likelihood of attaining his goal of extending Scrum's reach.

He also considered the level of support for Scrum within each business unit taking part in the pilots. A major factor in the success of the CRM project had been the significant support of Kristen and her team for both the project and for Scrum. Not all projects would be able to garner the same level of support, but it was nevertheless important to include such projects in order to show the extent to which Scrum could make a difference.

After examining the projects that fit these new criteria, he selected five projects with varying levels of importance and from different business units. Among these projects were those similar to the first pilot project, as well as more complex projects. One of the projects, for example, involved more than one business unit. The challenge of this project (related to alternative distribution channels) lay in the need to ensure that each of the business units were working together as a unified team so as to attain mutually satisfactory results. Hakan believed that Scrum had the potential to make a profound impact on this highly complex project. Proving its success would gain support from multiple business units and allow for radical change.

The day of their meeting had come, and it began with everyone briefly introducing their project proposals. Everyone except Mei had come to the meeting with a few proposals in mind. Evan and Hakan had selected some of the same projects, but in order to reveal Scrum's technical infrastructure aspects, Hakan had also chosen a project in which the client would be the IT department, itself. With Kristen's proposal also on the table, there were a total of seven different potential projects. This number seemed excessive to Mei, who felt that things were moving too fast and that it was too early to take on so many projects without thoroughly proving the efficacy of the Scrum framework. Therefore, she suggested selecting just a few of these propositions.

Kristen's project proposal was a crucial one and due to start imminently, and because no objections were raised, hers was the first project to be selected. The second project which was easily agreed upon was Evan's project for his own IT unit. In addition to these two projects, Hakan insisted that the project related to alternative distribution channels should also be included as a pilot. Everyone seemed to be happy with his proposal except Mei, whose primary concern was with the risks involved in applying this new method to a project involving multiple business units, but Hakan was determined to prove that this was in fact a positive factor. With its high level of complexity, the project was a priority for top management, and he saw it as an opportunity to prove the viability of Scrum and gain beneficial experience. Success on a project of this magnitude would not only impress management but could also potentially raise the overall interest in Scrum within the company.

With Hakan's resolve and Evan's support, Mei finally agreed to include the alternative distribution channels project in the piloting. Another smaller project that was not significantly important for management—also suggested by Hakan—was selected. The business unit involved in this last project had been difficult to work with in the past, so including it would challenge them to test the success of Scrum in yet another way. This brought the total number of approved pilot projects to four.

The meeting was progressing well, and everyone seemed prepared and genuinely enthusiastic about Scrum's potential to bring greater efficiency to operations, as well as to enhance communication and productivity. The matter of who would take the role of Scrum Master had yet to be discussed. Evan brought the issue to the table: "Obviously Hakan is well suited to this role, but if we expand Scrum's implementation throughout the company, we'll need more than one Scrum Master, as it would be very difficult for him to take responsibility for all of the projects. The workload would be too great. Therefore, along with considering Hakan, we should also evaluate a few new Scrum Master candidates. For example, the Scrum Master for our project could be someone from our own department." Nobody objected to Evan's proposal that new Scrum Masters should be trained alongside Hakan, but it seemed a bit strange to some of the others that he wanted to recruit a Scrum Master from within his own department. Hakan responded: "Evan, I absolutely agree with you. Obviously, we need new Scrum Masters to take on these new pilots, and we need to prepare for future projects involving Scrum. I would be happy to support and guide the new Scrum Masters in their roles, and I also feel positive about the Scrum Master being one of the team members in your project. If we can find someone who is willing and able to fulfill this role, we can try it. I will of course work closely with them to ensure that the process runs smoothly, and if we encounter any unexpected problems, we can always intervene accordingly."

Kristen agreed that things proceed as suggested, as long as Hakan took on the role of Scrum Master for her own project; she enjoyed working with him and felt that his input would be extremely valuable. Mei, on the other hand, seemed annoyed because she couldn't understand why Evan wanted them to exclude themselves from their own proposed projects. She didn't seem to fully understand the role of Scrum Master and felt that if s/he wasn't going to be someone from her own team, then a project manager must be assigned. Hakan reassured her that he would be tracking the progress and practice of each of the Scrum Masters, so the projects would still be under the control of her department, the PMO. He clarified that Project Managers from her team would work alongside the Scrum Masters to deliver the desired results. Mei clearly still had concerns about the way things would work, but she ultimately accepted the four pilot projects and proposals concerning the Scrum Master's role. After all, she would be able to intervene through Hakan when needed.

Hakan realized that he would need to work hard to convince the relevant business units of the benefits of adopting the Scrum framework for their projects. Leaving the meeting, he and Evan had already begun discussing each project's team structure.

Six months later

Nearly six months later, the CRM project had ended, and the second pilot project, involving Kristen's team, was almost over. Significant achievements had been attained in all of the pilot projects, whether completed or ongoing.

One of the projects was completed a month before the scheduled deadline, and with an underspend of 30% below its budget, proved to be an unprecedented success that would have been inconceivable using traditional project management methods. The results of the related surveys confirmed that the business units in all projects—including those in the project related to alternative distribution channels—were extremely satisfied with the outcomes of Scrum. Quality had also increased considerably; projects were less erroneous and more flexible, and the instant change requirements from the business units had been realized faster than before.

The advantages of the Scrum framework were undeniable, and news of its successes spread rapidly throughout the company. Hakan's hard work and persistence in delivering the new concept was paying off, and he knew he could leverage this newfound interest to maintain and spread the impetus of change.

Hakan set about working on the Transformation Action List to consolidate results and set targets for the short and medium terms. To date, five Scrum projects had either been completed or were still ongoing, and having experienced the benefits of working with Scrum, the business units and IT department were keen to use this new way of working in other potential areas.

Two additional Scrum Masters were training alongside Hakan in the pilot projects, but this was still not enough for him, as gradual implementation and steady progression were not what he envisaged for the rollout of Scrum throughout the company. He felt that effective and lasting change could only be achieved by increasing the number of teams using Scrum principles. Hakan felt that having to continually reintroduce the process to each team without applying the experience gained so far would not be effective. In order not to repeat the same mistakes or waste additional time and effort, their previous Scrum experience would need to be applied more actively by each new team. Accordingly, he began to think of solutions to ensure that all of the knowledge and experience gained in Scrum Teams could be shared.

Hakan's first solution was to motivate teams to regularly attend other Sprint events so that they could all learn from each other's varying practices, mistakes, and successes. This would lead to a feedback loop between teams, enabling collaborative learning through shared practice.

In order to improve cohesion and cooperation, Scrum Masters could also meet regularly to share their leadership experiences and support each other in sharing the problems and solutions they encountered. An information sharing platform could also be created at a later stage in order to ensure the continued development of Scrum Master practice, as well as to provide a forum for observations and feedback between teams, thereby further increasing competency and raising standards.

With the help of other Scrum Masters, the next step would be to create a roadmap to allow quick and easy rollout for teams new to the process. In this way, the speed of adaptation to change could be improved based on the lessons learned so far. This would allow them to determine new practices and standards for Scrum Teams, as well as to come up with ideas about how support could be provided to these new teams during the Scrum implementation process.

In order to set standards, a study would be conducted to determine how best to measure the performance of Scrum Teams. Currently, the only available performance metrics were the existing company performance criteria, which were essentially unsuited to the new, team-based approach. Their old system was based on the primacy of the individual, while Scrum relied on the formation of self-organizing, productive teams, and continuous, unified, collective improvement—it was definitely time to update the way they see and evaluate performance.

Apart from setting these new standards and providing supportive guidance to the teams, Hakan still felt he had more to do to raise the profile of Scrum, maintain momentum, and further encourage Scrum principles throughout the company. Their immense success achieved through the pilot projects would enable him to act more aggressively towards accelerating change, but he couldn't do it alone. The support of his fellow Scrum Masters, Evan, and the other executives convinced of the efficacy of Scrum would be essential in making his voice heard by top company executives and in convincing them of the need for fundamental change.

Formulating these ideas for the Transformation Action List was exhausting. Leaning back in his chair, he looked over the goals he had identified and thought about what he actually wanted all this to lead to. Hakan's goal was to create a Scrum Studio[22], a completely independent organization from (but still within) the company. With this new development, Studio teams could continually develop Scrum projects, driving results and acting independently of the clumsy, non-Scrum units that remained. Over time, with the Studio's inclusion of more people, it had the potential to transform the entire IT department. But even this would not be enough—his vision was to bring a totally new, Agile culture to the entire company, gaining acceptance across the board— not just within the IT unit, and not just for software projects. The ultimate goal was to evolve the existing giant, function-based, cumbersome organization into a self-organized, team-based, Agile network organization of start-ups. Looking at the updated Transformation Action List, it was obvious that it would take several years to get to this point.

It had been nearly a year since he and Mei had first discussed the possibility of introducing Scrum to the company, and so many things had changed in the lives of Hakan and the teams he had worked with since then. They had overcome many difficulties and unforgettable battles in the name of change. Hakan sighed—it had been a long year with extraordinary successes, but he knew that there were many more challenges ahead.

The real adventure was just about to begin...

---

[22] *Scrum Studio: Schwaber, Ken and Jeff Sutherland, Software in 30 Days (Hoboken, New Jersey: John Wiley & Sons, Inc., 2012)*

TRANSFORMATION ACTION LIST

TARGET	ACTION
Triggering knowledge and experience sharing between Scrum teams	Motivate teams to attend other teams' regular Sprint events
	Scrum Masters' regular gathering
	Information sharing platform
Making adaptation to change easier for new teams	New team rollout steps and supportive actions
	New, team-based performance system
Building competency	External team coaching support
	Scrum Master training
	Training on Agile technical practices for the Development Team
Scaling transformation	Continue experience sharing events within the company
	Continue surveys to track satisfaction levels
	Look for new potential Scrum implementation
Establish Scrum Studio	
Agile, network organization	

Appendices

Concepts and definitions
(Resource: https://guntherverheyen.com/scrum-glossary/)

Daily Scrum: A daily event, time-boxed to 15 minutes or less, to re-plan the development work during a Sprint. The event serves for the Development Team to share the daily progress, plan the work for the next 24 hours and update the Sprint Backlog accordingly.

Definition of Done: The set of expectations on quality that a product Increment must exhibit to make it releasable, i.e. fit for a release to the product's users.

Development Team: The group of people accountable for all evolutionary development work needed to create a releasable Increment no later than by the end of a Sprint.

Done: No known work remaining.

Increment: A body of releasable work that adds to and changes previously created Increments, and-as a whole-forms a product.

Kaizen: The perspective of continuous improvement for any current situation. Change for a better, continuous improvement mindset. (Japanese "kai": change, "zen": good, better).

Product Backlog: An ordered, evolving list of all work deemed necessary by the Product Owner to create, deliver, maintain, and sustain a product.

Product Backlog Refinement: The recurring activity in a

Sprint through which the Product Owner and the Development Team add granularity to future Product Backlog.

Product Owner: The person accountable for optimizing the value a product delivers, primarily by managing and expressing product functions and solutions in a Product Backlog. The single representative of all stakeholders and consumers.

Scrum: A simple framework that enables people to derive value from complex challenges.

Scrum Master: The person accountable for fostering an environment of Scrum by guiding, coaching, teaching and facilitating one or more Scrum Teams and their environment in understanding and employing Scrum.

Scrum Studio: An autonomous organizational unit, independent of the company organization, where people and teams apply Scrum principles.

Scrum Team: The team consisting of Scrum Master, Product Owner, and Development Team.

Sprint: An event that serves as a container for the other Scrum events, time-boxed to four weeks or less. The event serves getting a sufficient amount of work done, while ensuring timely inspection, reflection and adaptation at a product and strategic level. The other Scrum events are Sprint Planning, Daily Scrum, Sprint Review, and Sprint Retrospective.

Sprint Backlog / Scrum Board: An evolving plan of all work deemed necessary by the Development Team to realize a Sprint's goal. Mostly represented via the Scrum Board.

Sprint Burndown Chart: A chart showing the decrease of remaining work against time.

Sprint Goal: A concise statement expressing the overarching purpose of a Sprint.

Sprint Planning Event (Planning Event): An event marking the start of a Sprint, time-boxed to eight hours or less. The event serves for the Scrum Team to inspect the Product Backlog considered most valuable at that time and design that forecast into an initial Sprint Backlog against the Sprint Goal.

Sprint Retrospective Event (Retrospective Event): An event marking the closing of a Sprint, time-boxed to three hours or less. The event serves for the Scrum Team to inspect the Sprint that is ending and establish the way of working for the next Sprint.

Sprint Review Event (Review Event): An event marking the closing of the development of a Sprint, time-boxed to four hours or less. The event serves for the Scrum Team and the stakeholders to inspect the Increment, the overall progress and strategic changes in order to allow the Product Owner to update the Product Backlog.

Sprint Velocity: Popular indication of the average amount of Product Backlog turned into an Increment of releasable product during a Sprint by a specific (composition of) a team.

Story/User Story: Product Backlog Item, a potential feature to be added to the product.

Transformation Action List: A list of items that should be acted on to ensure successful implementation and widespread use of Scrum.

Timebox: A container in time of a maximum duration, potentially a fixed duration. In Scrum, all events have a maximum duration only, except for the Sprint itself, which has a fixed duration.

Daily Scrum Checklist

Have you and the Scrum(s) recognized any change in the total delivery time of your demands?	Delivering much faster	Delivering faster	Did not change	Delivering slower	Delivering much slower
In case of business priority or demand change, have you recognized any change in the response time of the Scrum team(s)?	Responding much faster	Responding faster	Did not change	Responding slower	Responding much slower
Have your business requirements been implemented as you demanded?	Requirements are implemented without need for correction	Requirements are implemented in a more accurate way	There were no changes	We occasionally encounter problems on requirements and ask for correction	We frequently encounter problems on requirements and ask for correction
Apart from the demands you directly requested from the Scrum team(s), do you think that the Srum team(s) contribute to business goals by putting extra value-added solutions into place?	Always	Often	Sometimes	Seldom	Never
Compared to other projects, how do you view the quality level of the projects developed by the Scrum team(s)?	Much better	Better	No change	Worse	Much worse
Are you happy with the Scrum way of working?	Always	Often	Sometimes	Seldom	Never

Business Satisfaction Survey

No:	Questions	Yes/No
1	Occurs at the same time and place	
2	No one arrives late, begins on time	
3	All team members attend	
4	The meeting lasts fifteen minutes or less	
5	High energy and morale (at the end, team members have a plan for the day and are excited to begin)	
6	All team members are prepared for the meeting	
7	No one facilitates the meeting, the team is self-organized	
8	Assists in team building (everyone cares about what the others are working on)	
9	Everyone communicates clearly about status & progress	
10	Team shares a commitment, remembering and reinforcing their Sprint Goal	
11	Impediments are identified	
12	Team works offline to solve problems	
13	Team members are comfortable sharing problems and impediments	
14	All team members listen to each other	
15	Observers (if any) listen to the team without intervention	
16	Scrum Board is updated	

www.ingramcontent.com/pod-product-compliance
Lightning Source LLC
Chambersburg PA
CBHW050002230526
45465CB00003BB/1229